D0175530

How to Love

Also by Gordon Livingston

Only Spring:
On Mourning the Death of My Son

Too Soon Old, Too Late Smart:
Thirty True Things You Need to Know Now

And Never Stop Dancing:
Thirty More True Things You Need to Know Now

How to Love

Gordon Livingston, M.D.

Da Capo
∞
LIFE
LONG

A Member of the Perseus Books Group

DESIGN BY JANE RAESE
Set in 12-point Dante

Cataloging-in-Publication data for this book is available from the Library of Congress.

First Da Capo Press edition 2009
ISBN 978-0-7382-1280-7

Published by Da Capo Press
A Member of the Perseus Books Group
www.dacapopress.com

Da Capo Press books are available at special discounts for bulk purchases in the U.S. by corporations, institutions, and other organizations. For more information, please contact the Special Markets Department at the Perseus Books Group, 2300 Chestnut Street, Suite 200, Philadelphia, PA, 19103, or call (800) 810-4145, ext. 5000, or e-mail special.markets@perseusbooks.com.

10 9 8 7 6 5 4 3 2 1

To Clare

Who taught me all I know about love
and still trusts me enough to fall asleep beside me.

Contents

Acknowledgments   xi

First deserve, then desire.   xiii

Oh, how powerfully the magnet of illusion
attracts.   xxv

1   *A Man Is Known by the Company He Avoids*

Don't blame the mirror for your own
reflection.   5

Fear is the prison of the heart.   25

Always borrow from a pessimist; he won't expect
to be paid back.   34

No hell is private.   51

Against boredom the gods themselves
fight in vain.   55

The best of compasses does not point
to true north.   61

Contents

We cannot direct the wind but we can
trim the sails.   64

Life is rarely as simple as we would have it.   69

We flatter ourselves if we believe that our
character is fixed.   75

What is essential is invisible to the eye.   80

The first duty of love is to listen.   85

When all is said and done, more is said
than done.   88

2 *People to Cherish*

The Essential Virtues   95

Kindness   98

Optimism   103

Courage   108

Loyalty   114

Tolerance   118

Honesty   122

Contents

Beauty   126

Humor   132

Flexibility   136

Intelligence   138

3 *It Is Not the Answer That Enlightens but the Question*

The most dangerous food to eat is a wedding cake.   143

The gods too are fond of a joke: the role of chance in human affairs.   148

Love will make you forget time and time will make you forget love.   152

Any landing you can walk away from is a good landing.   158

Falling in love with love is falling for make-believe.   164

Experience: Test first, lesson later.   169

Contents

The trouble with parents is that by the time
they are experienced they are unemployed.   173

If it weren't for marriage, men and women
would have to fight with total strangers.   179

Beware of those who are sure they are right.   185

Money can't buy happiness; it can, however,
rent it.   187

Ideas are easier to love than people.   192

If you were arrested for kindness, would there
be enough evidence to convict?   196

About the Author   205

Acknowledgments

Any book on a subject as complex as love depends on borrowed thoughts. While many of the interpretations contained herein are my own, I have relied on the numberless contributions of members of my profession who have help organize the descriptions of human behavior into the patterns described in the Diagnostic and Statistical Manual of the American Psychiatric Association. Like our Constitution, this is an evolving document that is on the verge of its fifth edition. I have not named any of the many people who have enlarged our understanding of personality structure and you can be sure that in their next books they will not name me.

Matthew Lore, my longtime editor and friend, played a major role in encouraging the birth of this book. John Radziewicz directed its completion with an astute editorial eye and a kind heart. The rest of the hospitable and hard-working Da Capo staff have been supportive and efficient. My agent, Rafe Sagalyn, again provided invaluable guidance through the frequently confusing world of publishing.

Acknowledgments

My daughter Emily, when not defending the rights of the accused of Montgomery County, Maryland, applied her considerable discernment to reading early drafts of the manuscript. Her mother Clare remains my model for the virtues of those we seek to cherish.

First deserve, then desire.

The choices we make, choices on which our happiness largely depends, involve judgments about the people we encounter as we travel through life. Whom can we trust? Who will bring out the best in us? Who will betray us? Who will save us from ourselves? These judgments are important in direct proportion to the closeness of the relationship. If we are deceived by a salesperson, we have lost only money. If we give our hearts to someone unworthy of the gift, we lose more than we can afford.

To be in the presence of another person who accepts us as we are, gives us the benefit of the doubt, cares what we think, and assumes we will act generously is an immensely gratifying experience. We are drawn to such people, both because they are unusual and because they encourage us toward similar behavior. If someone treats us this way consistently we come to love them, sometimes in spite of ourselves.

We do not choose our families. We are fortunate if we spend our formative years with people who are reliable sources of affection, kindness, and self-control. Not all of us are this lucky, and so we frequently emerge into adult-hood burdened by certain interpersonal habits and self-esteem deficits that we either overcome or pass on to a new generation of children. At some point as grown-ups, we learn that our behaviors define us more than any thoughts or feelings we might experience. In other words, *we are what we do.* And we begin to make choices about who we want to be and whom we want to be with.

Each of us carries around a picture in our minds of the perfect life partner. Sometimes, of course, this fantasy is just a mirror image of ourselves that allows for certain physical dissimilarities. In other cases the desired person will be the repository of all the qualities that we admire but lack. This complementary image can often be re-duced to a list of attributes that we imagine will make someone perfect for us. As we encounter people, we match them to our mental lists to decide if we want to see more of them. The person we finally fall in love with tends, in the end, to be similar to us in most important re-spects, including intelligence, social class, and shared in-terests. "Like marries like" is the rule of thumb. Along the way to finding this person, we typically have our hearts broken a time or two. But we push on until we en-counter someone who has most of the traits we think are important and who agrees for his or her own reasons to link their life to ours.

Then, over time, we become bored if we're lucky, antagonistic if we're not. The love of our youth becomes the bane of our middle age. If you think this formulation is overly cynical, look around you. How many of the established marriages with which you are familiar would you describe as fulfilling? And you are sampling only unions that have survived, so far.

"People change over time" is the usual explanation for falling out of love with the person to whom we promised eternal fidelity. And who can deny it? We are not the people we were yesterday, much less who we were ten or twenty years ago. And yet, how many of us change our fundamental beliefs and personalities as we age? It seems to me that there is a deeper problem in evaluating people and what they will become. We are simply not trained to think in terms of constellations of character traits and what they imply in terms of both compatibility and future conduct.

How much easier would it all be if we were more like our major appliances and came with owner's manuals, full of useful information on how to operate our bodies and spirits in efficient, pleasure-inducing ways. If there were such a manual it would surely contain a chapter on *how to recognize people to be wary of and people to cherish.*

In my experience as a therapist, I have found that the pitfalls most people encounter in their pursuit of happiness reflect some difficulty in apprehending what is "true" about themselves and the people they are closest to. We are, in effect, navigating with faulty maps of how the world works. To correct these maps does not require therapy. Most people find their way by trial and error. The problem with this approach, beyond the randomness of its outcomes, is that our lives are finite. Each of us has an indeterminate but limited time to figure out how to navigate accurately. And many people show a peculiar tendency to replicate rather than correct mistakes. Whether this is just a testimony to the power of habit or the triumph of hope over experience is unclear.

What we must learn to do is look beneath the surface of our lives and recognize that much of what we are depends on emotions and motivations outside our consciousness; these feelings reside in the realm of long, unexamined habit. Our personal styles are simply the usual way we interact with others. And the paradox is this: *Our greatest strengths are our greatest weaknesses.* Even our capacity for love can betray us; taken to obsessive extremes, it can beget something very like hate.

First deserve, then desire.

In our attempts to find happiness and surround ourselves with people who will help us reach this goal, we are faced with the elemental truth that *we are entitled to receive only what we are prepared to give.* Most of us eventually realize that the person of our dreams, even if we are lucky enough to find him or her, will have their own needs and desires that we may or may not be able to satisfy. This is why it is important to cultivate in ourselves those traits of character that we value in others. And given our human fallibility, the most important quality may turn out to be the ability to forgive.

It is our ability to apprehend and integrate into our lives certain important truths about human relationships that determines how successful our searches for lasting intimacy will be. For example, it is not evident to many people that *the fundamental requirement for any satisfying relationship is a reciprocal ability to see the world as others see it, to be able to put ourselves in someone else's shoes.* Once we recognize that empathy is a primary virtue on which our happiness depends, we can begin to develop an appreciation of this noble characteristic. This effort might be called *becoming the person you long to love.* All of life's most important searches, whether for material success, enlightenment, or the perfect partner, turn out to be journeys within.

First deserve, then desire.

How do we learn to make intelligent judgments about others? Who is qualified to teach us? Our parents would be obvious choices. They have, after all, lived in the world longer than we. Surely they have learned something from their own mistakes and successes that will enlighten us. That this does not happen routinely is a commentary on how uncertain is the task of parenting. We cannot teach what we do not know. And so powerful is the force of habit that what passes for conscious living often is simply repeating the same behaviors to which we are accustomed — whether they are working or not. It was said of an airline pilot that, though his logbook showed 30,000 flying hours, they were just the same hour 30,000 times. As much can be said of many of our lives.

If not from our parents, from whom are we supposed to learn? Adolescence is the most accelerated period for acquiring social skills and developing a beginning sense of who we are and where we are going. If we look closely at where teenagers acquire their knowledge about the world, we are discouraged to learn that they depend mostly on their peers and what they observe on televisions, computers, and movie screens. Some printed information makes it through, but even this consists largely of publications devoted to what might be called the celebrity culture.

Guidance from peers in one's teenage years can charitably be termed unreliable (sometimes referred to as "the blond leading the blond"). If you don't believe me, spend a little time on MySpace.com. The values portrayed and the relationships apparently formed there do not make one optimistic about the future. Nor is popular culture edifying with regard to the large questions of meaning. Beyond narrow definitions of beauty, the behaviors exhibited by our entertainment icons are undependable guides to how to live happily in the world.

In the overheated, hormonally driven environment of high school, accidental attributes such as physical attractiveness and athletic ability are overvalued. Those who possess neither of these characteristics tend to inhabit the margins. Anyone who has been back to their twentieth high school reunion can attest that other qualities such as intelligence and a capacity for hard work wear better as life goes along. But even these admirable traits may not correlate closely with feelings of success and personal satisfaction.

Happiness, like art, can be difficult to define, but it is clear that an essential component of a fulfilling life is the quality of our closest relationships. People living in good marriages not only report higher levels of satisfaction with their lives, they live longer.

One would think, therefore, that every high school curriculum would contain at least one course devoted to forming and sustaining close relationships. That this is not the case would suggest either that there is not a body of knowledge that would assist us in our efforts to seek intimacy with others or that we are all expected to learn this skill elsewhere. It is apparent from the divorce rate, hovering around fifty percent, that the latter assumption cannot be reliable.

There is, however, a store of organized, validated, and teachable information about human behavior and personality. Descriptions in the psychological literature show that certain traits, for example kindness and dependability, appear to coexist, just as do less desirable characteristics like cruelty and dishonesty. If this is true, we can begin to describe people in more or less accurate ways in terms of habitual behaviors. This is important because everything we do represents a communication about ourselves and what we value. There is also a predictive usefulness to learning to extrapolate traits that we infer from observing others. *The best guide we have to future behavior is past behavior.* This is, after all, a primary basis for our system of laws and incarceration. (It is also an answer to the question: How can we judge a person by the worst thing he has ever done?)

First deserve, then desire.

If we wish, therefore, to protect ourselves from disappointment at the hands of others, and if we think it important to recognize those who will enrich our lives, we had best learn the art of *pattern recognition* when it comes to human behavior. That this has traditionally proven difficult is both a problem of education — who can teach us this and where? — and a testimony to the complexity of human needs. We are not simply creatures of intellect who make decisions based on logic and experience. We are also sentient beings in the grip of conflicting needs, impulses, and fears: sexual, affectional, social, religious, parental, and, above all, self-protective. The fight or flight mechanism is our evolutionary heritage and the stakes have become far more than simply physical survival. For most of us, humiliation represents a kind of death.

It must be said about any collection of personality traits that they seldom exist in pure form. This is why labeling people is dangerous. In our effort to generalize about certain styles we are always at risk of overlooking the complexity that characterizes each of our personalities. The truth is that *we are all capable of exhibiting attributes that cause us difficulty.* Who among us is not prone to impulsive mistakes, self-centered conduct, rapid mood changes, and poorly controlled anger? If we are to understand and manage these behaviors, it helps us to recognize why they are maladaptive and what happens at the extremes of disordered personalities.

So the purpose of these analyses is not to separate ourselves from others whom we can never be like. The object is to recognize what traits and behaviors get us more of what we want in life — happiness — and less of what we seek to avoid — emotional pain, especially loneliness. To have more of the former and less of the latter, it is important to surround ourselves with people with whom we can share a mutual affection and admiration.

This is, in part, a cautionary book. It does not concern itself with treatment for the conditions it describes. This is not meant to be a pessimistic commentary on people's capacity for transformation. Most of my professional life has been involved in efforts to promote such change. What I have learned in that time is that resolving symptoms such as anxiety, depression, even delusions, is usually a lot easier than changing someone's personality. Our habitual ways of interacting with other people are notoriously hard to alter even if one has the time and resources to devote to extended psychotherapy. How much harder it is then to change these ingrained traits in someone who does not see them as problematic and prefers to view interpersonal difficulties as the fault of others. This is not a job for civilians. The romantic idea that we can fundamentally change another person with our love and support is a dream seldom realized.

Some may be put off at the idea of avoiding rather than helping or accommodating people with problems that are embedded in their personalities. If you are already enmeshed in a relationship with such a person or are a fellow family member, you may need help that you will not find here. My descriptions are directed at relationships of choice, which turn out to be critical to our pursuit of happiness. If you discover a relative in the "people to be wary of" section, perhaps this will at least explain what happened at that last Thanksgiving dinner.

There is much debate about the origins of personality problems. To what extent are they genetic? How much can we attribute to poor parenting or adverse life experience? The answer, dimly seen at the moment, is probably some of each. In a way, though, this is beside the point. If our pleasure and satisfaction in this life are connected to our closest relationships, what we really need to know is how to recognize those who are worthy of our trust and affection and how to steer clear of those who will ultimately disappoint us, waste our time, and break our hearts and spirits.

Of all the questions we ask ourselves in the course of discovering what another human being is really like, perhaps the most important is this: *How do I feel about myself when I am with this person?*

What follows, then, are two contrasting sets of descriptions. The first part of the book is a more or less systematic summary of personality types who are likely to hurt us. The second is an explication of the virtues we seek in others even as we try to develop them in ourselves. The third is concerned with the relationships we form and how to improve them. As in all things, "the wisdom to know the difference" draws us onward.

*Oh, how powerfully the magnet
of illusion attracts.*

It would seem that the personality styles that I will describe in Part I are so evidently unattractive that they would be easily recognized and that we would instinctively recoil from them. That this is not true and that many of us are, in fact, drawn to people whom we later come to despise is a tribute to the concept of paradox and our confusion about what traits wear well through the passing years.

We are, for example, fascinated by movie stars and the world that they inhabit. The closest that most of us will come to meeting such people are the shallow and theatrical, often physically attractive, persons whom we encounter in our own lives. They inhabit our adolescent fantasies. Unencumbered by an inclination to reflect on their actions, they tend to be socially adept and entertaining. They are more likely to be on the cheerleading squad than in the math club. They fit our youthful concept of what it means to be beautiful, and their habitual impulsivity can be interpreted as an appealing spontaneity, especially by those whose efforts at achieving pleasure are inhibited. Only over time does their superficiality and lack of organization become a problem. An inability to be on time and a poor sense of direction may be seen as charming foibles early in a relationship. Long-term, we all need to be able to balance our checkbooks.

Self-centered people frequently seem successful. Their ability to get others to conform to their opinions and satisfy their needs may appear to be a valuable life skill; over time these qualities are revealed as manipulative and a lack of interest in the needs of others becomes a highly unattractive trait. An observer may be confused by an ability to feign emotions that the self-absorbed do not feel. Pretending to listen, for example, is a behavior easily learned by those who have discovered that the primary organs of seduction are the ears.

A certain amount of uncertainty about what we are looking for in others is inevitable. In a society that values competition, we are expected to get what we want without being too obvious about it. To take one example, the males among us frequently come to believe that the satisfaction of their sexual needs requires a fair amount of dissembling, especially if you happen to be a teenaged boy in the grip of what might generously be described as a preoccupation with the subject. It is disorienting to discover that the attitudes of society in general and girls in particular place serious constraints on one's desire to have sex as promiscuously as possible.

The suppression of this drive is important because it occurs at a time when we are trying out new ways of relating to others and feeling dishonest about our need to feel sexually adequate while conforming our behavior to some approximation of the golden rule. The resolution of this conflict colors a lot of our future ability to balance our own desires with the needs of those whose affection and good opinion are crucial to our happiness.

Unfortunately, the lesson that many of us learn from this period in our lives is that power in any relationship depends on a kind of win/lose negotiation in which our gain is at someone else's expense. This also leads to the concept of compromise as an essential element of the negotiation. Neither party is expected to get everything they want, which dovetails nicely with the "nobody's perfect" idea that is an article of faith among those in bad relationships (who then sometimes presume to teach us how to be happy).

In fact, the kind of negotiation that is intended to produce the best outcome for ourselves at the expense of others is the very antithesis of *love, that emotion that places the needs and desires of another at the level of our own.* If no one teaches us this definition, and if we have been surrounded by self-centered people, we are likely to be most attuned to our own needs and adopt a view of relationships in which other people are seen as supporting players in the life drama in which we are the stars. This tendency is reinforced by stories we tell ourselves about what it means to be successful in this culture with its emphasis on consumption and materialism as primary pathways to happiness.

The negotiation of sexual needs leads to a lot of resentment, particularly on the part of young men who often feel themselves relatively powerless. Women are able to exercise control by giving and withholding sex, which, in general, has a different meaning for them than it does for men. (There is some truth to the old saw that "Women need a reason to have sex; men just need a place.") It is not surprising then that these biological urges are the source of a lot of cynicism and manipulativeness on both sides of the gender divide at a juncture in life when everyone is feeling uneasy about what sort of person they want to be and whom they want to draw close to.

And where can we turn for guidance in these matters? Our families may or may not provide environments in which to observe healthy and satisfying adult relationships. Usually, not so much. Even intact families have a lot of conflict. "All couples fight" is a cultural truism, as is the belief that sibling rivalry is inevitable. In fact, these ideas are subsets of the "Life is hard, then you die" concept that keeps everyone's expectations low and serves as a rationalization for a lot of unhappiness. Most of what we hear about parenting, in fact, is that raising children is a burdensome and expensive task, fraught with anxiety as kids pass though a series of unattractive stages: demanding infant, terrible twos, ungrateful preteen, and acting out adolescent. The concept of sacrificial parenthood is a staple of the culture. And, as always, our expectations tend to be realized.

So most of us are raised to believe several things that militate against closeness to others. For example, love is conditional and subject to competition. (Corollary: If you want unqualified approval, get a dog.) Second, an unspoken and revocable *contract* is at the heart of even our closest relationships. (I will do certain things that you want if you will reciprocate.) Third, everything is negotiable, so that the satisfaction of needs depends heavily on the same skills that succeed in business, notably an ability to "sell yourself." Perhaps the most significant lesson that we take away from our families is the transience of all things human: Nothing very good or very bad lasts very long.

How does this set of beliefs affect the development of our personalities, the collections of traits and habitual ways of relating to others that define us as people? First of all, these ideas are based on the assumption that people operate largely on their conceptions of their own self-interest. In addition, it can be assumed that behaviors that are rewarded will be repeated while those that are not will be extinguished. Psychologically, this is the "animal trainer" model used to shape behavior in astonishing ways in circuses and aquariums.

Since humans are less responsive to simple reinforcers like food, our relationship behaviors are learned using more complicated incentives: some positive, such as money or peer approval, and some negative, like loneliness and humiliation. What we seldom do in this trial-and-error process of developing a personal style is to examine our basic assumptions about what people are like and how to satisfy our uniquely human need to live lives that contain both pleasure and meaning. We quickly discover that we cannot do this alone. We require the good opinion of a few others and we long for the unconditional love of at least one.

Not what you have, but what you use;
Not what you see, but what you choose;
Not what seems fair, but what is true;
Not what you dream, but what you do;
Not what you take, but what you give;
Not as you pray, but as you live.
These are the things that mar or bless
The sum of human happiness.

—Author Unknown

1

A Man Is Known
by the Company He Avoids

Groucho Marx memorably observed that, "I would never join a club that would have someone like me as a member." Those we choose to spend time with define both who we think we are and who we want to be. They must be chosen carefully.

The formal definition of a so-called personality disorder is as follows: "An enduring pattern of inner experience and behavior that deviates markedly from cultural expectations, is pervasive and inflexible, is stable over time, and leads to distress and functional impairment." People who have these collections of traits in diagnosable form are extremely difficult to relate to and especially to live with. I am going to describe several categories of such people because recognizing how these habitual attitudes and behaviors coexist is important. This knowledge will help us understand why these personality types are resistant to change and the ways they can adversely influence the emotional well-being of those around them. These are the people your mother warned you about — or should have. You allow them into your life at great risk.

*Don't blame the mirror for
your own reflection.*

People who are self-absorbed can be dangerous emotionally and sometimes even physically. As a species we are programmed to act in our own self-interest. Survival of the fittest is an evolutionary imperative. Our capitalist system has elevated this need into the most powerful economic engine ever devised. That said, those among us who are *only* for themselves cause the rest of us a lot of problems.

The most benign form of self-absorption is manifested by so-called histrionic people, who often describe themselves as "passionate and emotional." Their primary drive is to be the center of attention and they populate our television and movie screens. Primarily female, they are the "drama queens" whose physical attributes and seductiveness have come to occupy the fantasies of millions of boys and men. The emulation of this style by some girls and women causes problems for those of us who are unlikely to be dating any Hollywood starlets.

The sexually provocative dress and mannerisms that are the bane of middle and high school administrators are testimonies to the enduring power of the cultural icons who occupy the pages of *People* and *Playboy* magazines. As long as we are socialized to admire persons like this we will be prone to overlook other, less desirable, traits that they manifest. Typically, people who display this style are emotionally shallow and unstable. Uninterested in details, their grasp of the world is impressionistic and theatrical. Their self-absorption and superficiality make it hard for them to engage in the give and take of healthy relationships. Their capacity for commitment is limited and is reflected in the brevity of many celebrity marriages.

Often such women gravitate toward connections with obsessive men who promise to provide the structure and organization that they characteristically lack. (The men in question are promised some much-needed entertainment.) These unions, while apparently complementary, infrequently endure. While opposites may attract, they seldom do well with each other in the long term. Even the sex, which appears to hold the most promise, is generally not fulfilling. Behind all that seductiveness is a tendency to use sexuality as an instrument of manipulation.

While we may try to convince ourselves that sex is primarily a physical and recreational act, it turns out that it just isn't that good in the absence of mutual caring and an ability to engage emotionally.

Danger signals that one is in the presence of a self-absorbed "hysteric" include signs of the aforementioned shallowness and a more or less constant need to be the focus of attention. Rapid shifts in emotionality are common, as are inappropriate displays of intimacy. Think of the flirtatious mannerisms of the highly seductive people whom we pay to entertain us. If the person you are with reminds you in appearance and behavior of a movie star you saw recently promoting her latest picture, look more closely for some of the other signs of superficiality and self-centeredness that would signal that she may be promising more than she can deliver. And remember what happened between Scarlett O'Hara and Rhett Butler.

Imagine living with someone who requires continual stimulation and admiration, who is incapable of serious thought and conversation, who is preoccupied with appearances (especially her own), and whose primary avocation is shopping. That such a person is commonly very attractive confuses men who have been socialized to pursue such women as the feminine ideal. At the same time, histrionic women have grown up believing that their conventional beauty is the most valuable thing about them and have become accustomed to using this to get what they want, particularly from men. They are poorly suited for long-term relationships and childrearing. It is just very hard for them to get beyond their own needs to consider their obligations to others, even their own children. The passage of time is especially unkind to them.

Like all of the self-absorbed personality types, the histrionic style appears to work for a time but ultimately fails as others in their lives become disillusioned. There is a scene in *Annie Hall* where Woody Allen is on a couch with a beautiful woman who talks about how open she is sexually. When finally he lunges and tries to kiss her she pushes him away. He looks into the camera and wonders, "How could I have misread the signals?" He is not alone.

Next up in the self-absorbed constellation are the narcissists. Narcissus, you will recall, was the beautiful but cold youth of Greek mythology who became so enamored of his reflection in a pool that he could not avert his eyes and wasted away contemplating his own image. In this category we have those who manifest such an elevated perception of themselves that they have little ability to hear heartbeats other than their own. They lack the capacity for that vital human characteristic, *empathy,* the ability to put ourselves emotionally in the place of another.

They are envious of others and imagine that others are envious of them. This characteristic raises an important question we all must confront: How large an audience are we performing for? Many people are so sensitive to the opinions of others that they are filled with anxiety and self-consciousness. At the extremes this can result in either paranoia or an exaggerated sense of one's own importance. The truth is that other people, intent on pursuing their own lives, have a limited interest in us. The few who love us care deeply, but to imagine that large numbers of others are noticing, much less judging, what we do is an unrealistic burden. If such attention becomes a self-centered need we are entering the unattractive world of conceit.

Unable to tolerate criticism, narcissists live in fear of humiliation. This causes them to be attuned to any hint of disapproval and they are prone to lash out when criticized. They manifest feelings of entitlement: The rules that apply to everyone else do not necessarily constrain them because of their sense of their own "specialness." In a traffic jam, they are the people in expensive cars passing on the shoulder. They are often preoccupied with fantasies of success, power, or beauty. They are, in a word, *arrogant*. They are also prepared to take advantage of others when it suits their needs.

People with strongly narcissistic traits do not tend to age gracefully. The losses and limitations that accompany the process of growing old and our societal preoccupation with youth mean that people with this form of self-absorption are overrepresented in bodybuilding gyms and in the offices of plastic surgeons.

The primary sign that one is in the presence of a narcissist is that *he or she is not interested in you except as a source of admiration.* Lacking real concern for others, they are notoriously bad listeners. A former New York City mayor is reported to have said to someone he was conversing with, "That's enough about me. Let's talk about you. What do you think of me?" Whether true or not, this statement conveys the essence of the narcissistic style: a preoccupation with self that conveys a belief that one is so important that everyone else is simply a member of the audience.

Narcissistic traits are among the unattractive features seen in many adolescents. This can be attributed to the focus on the self that is necessary to separate from one's family, the individuation that is an important task for this stage of life. It also reflects a sheltered inexperience with the humbling events with which life eventually confronts us all. Once we have had to deal with our share of losses and rejections, it becomes harder to imagine ourselves as centrally important and uniquely admired. Those adults afflicted with narcissism in many respects resemble self-centered teenagers who believe that the world does (or should) revolve around them.

Self-absorption linked to ambition describes the personality of many politicians. The higher the office, it seems, the more candidates are required to present themselves as paragons of wisdom and virtue. They become repositories of our best hopes that someone will emerge to take care of us, vanquish our enemies, and by their inspired leadership bring us together in a safe and happy world. To promise such a thing requires a self-confidence bordering on the delusional, which explains the underlying narcissism of many of our political stars whom we reward with our votes and with whom we eventually become disillusioned when they fail to fulfill their exaggerated promises and our unrealistic hopes.

It should not be hard to recognize people who manifest a grandiose sense of self-importance, and yet they cause untold heartache. Four out of five of them are male (hence the common complaint of women that the men in their lives are not listening to them). In a culture where physical attractiveness and self-confidence are highly valued, their glibness and stories of success are initially appealing. Commonly intelligent, they are able to feign interest in others so that their lack of empathy may take time to become apparent.

Think of those people you know who exhibit a sense that they are so special that they are outraged when anyone places constraints upon them, who have difficulty participating in conversations that do not center on them, and who convey in ways large and small the fact that everyone else exists primarily to meet their needs and desires. Recall the different ways that people on board the *Titanic* behaved when it was clear that the ship was sinking. "If we are not for ourselves, who will be? If we are only for ourselves, what are we?" Not good candidates for a lasting relationship, that's for sure.

A particularly vexing group of self-absorbed people to beware of are those with so-called "borderline" traits who are so impulsive, unpredictable, and unstable in their interactions with others that one never knows from moment to moment, day to day, how they will behave. These are people whose defining characteristic is an *in-*

tense fear of abandonment accompanied by such a tenuous control of their anger that they are prone to pyrotechnic emotional displays that leave those around them aghast with surprise and fury. In a moment they may go from idealizing someone to a bitter attack against them. Knowing where one stands with such a person is difficult, to say the least.

Underlying these confusing shifts in mood and allegiance is a shattered sense of self characterized by a pervasive feeling of emptiness and lack of a firm sense of identity. Solitude is intolerable. They may feel so devalued that they contemplate suicide, and they are prone to depression and self-destructive behaviors such as cutting themselves, promiscuity, eating disorders, or addictions to drugs. Three of four borderlines are women.

These people are full of surprises and are often identifiable simply because they are surrounded by emotional chaos. Those in their orbit often find *themselves* behaving in confusing and impulsive ways as a reaction to the sudden mood shifts of the borderline. Most confusing is the bitter and poorly controlled anger that borderlines exhibit. If you think about it, our attempts to make sense of the world and the people in it require a certain stability that allows us to anticipate what is likely to happen next. Imagine how difficult it would be to attempt to navigate in a universe in which the environment was constantly changing, in which hills became valleys and roads and buildings moved about randomly. Such is the emotional landscape of the borderline.

Their propensity for sudden mood shifts often results in an incorrect diagnosis of bipolar illness, in which more sustained changes of mood from mania to severe depression are seen. While bipolar persons can have rapidly cycling moods, they do not, in general, vacillate from euphoria to despair several times a day, as is common in borderlines.

No matter how satisfied with our lives we may be, most men welcome additional excitement, particularly if it comes in the form of a sexually appealing, apparently uninhibited woman. And especially if we find ourselves being assured that she finds us uniquely and irresistibly attractive. If, however, this intensely satisfying experience is followed by a certain clinginess and predictions that we will abandon her, we ought to be suspicious. If we throw in some episodes of inexplicable rage, threats or instances of self-harm, and indications of substance abuse, then misgivings about the relationship ought to result. Think about the Glenn Close character in *Fatal Attraction*.

Even psychotherapists, who presumably ought to know better, can be fooled. A woman came to my office complaining of depression. In the course of the first few sessions, she appeared to be doing better and assured me that I was the most skilled and caring therapist of the many with whom she had worked (all of whom, she told me, had ultimately failed her). Then one day she came in and disclosed that she had seen me jogging along a nearby country road and it was only with difficulty that she had resisted the impulse to swerve her car and run me down. I began to reevaluate both my diagnosis and jogging routes.

Because of their unstable self-image and difficulty controlling their mood, the lives of such people comprise a wasteland of discarded relationships. They carom from clinging dependency to angry manipulation. They alternate between unrealistic demands for attention and feelings of self-loathing. They leave anger and confusion in their wake and no one can be said to know them.

Because of their unpredictability they make especially poor parents. Children require for healthy development a relatively stable environment, physically and emotionally. Deprived of this by having a changeable, sometimes explosive, parent, they are at risk to develop the rudderless, poorly modulated personality characteristics that make it so hard to form secure, committed connections with others.

The typical childhood of a borderline has been described by one author as "a desolate battlefield." Chronic abuse or neglect is often present and they commonly have mothers who also fit the criteria for borderline personality. They are torn between a longing to merge and a fear of being swallowed up. Like most people with personality disorders, they are often oblivious to their behavior patterns and intolerant of criticism. What they evoke in others is most often anger, so they frequently experience some form of abandonment, which solidifies and validates their feelings of loss and betrayal.

You know you are in the presence of a borderline when you feel in danger of developing emotional whiplash from their sudden mood changes and their seemingly bottomless need for support. "I hate you, don't leave me" is the mantra of the borderline (and the title of one of the best books on the subject). Marry one and you risk a lifetime of confusion and unhappiness.

Finally we come to the sociopaths, a particularly dangerous category of people since they are deficient in that most important capacity that the rest of us take for granted as a fundamental component of what it is to be human: *conscience.* This is the internal moral compass that regulates our interactions with others. It is a sense of obligation based on our feelings of affection and attachment. It impels us to generosity and heroism, is the basis for empathy, and results in feelings of guilt or regret when we do things that harm another person. The restraining effects of conscience on our behavior do not depend on our assessment of whether we will be caught or punished. Rather we sense or have been taught that certain behaviors are wrong because they injure someone else or have a corrosive effect on the social compact that binds us together.

Apart from whatever ethical system or religious beliefs that govern our behavior, our conscience is an acknowledgment that we are part of society and that fairness requires us to treat other people as we expect to be treated. If we lack such conviction and instead see others only as objects to be manipulated for our own pleasure or gain, we are sociopaths and operating outside our culture's laws and norms. People like this, however they disguise their intentions, eventually come to be seen as missing some essential component of what it is to be human. They can do a lot of damage to those who link their lives to theirs.

The indications that one's conscience is operating can be observed in circumstances ranging from the trivial (a store clerk gives you too much change) to the consequential (you are presented with an opportunity to cheat on your spouse). How we react in these situations, whether we feel an intervening sense of obligation, devotion, or love, defines us as human beings. Like most personality traits, this ability to feel guilt or responsibility for our behavior exists on a continuum. We must learn to recognize the people at the lower end: the shameless, the ruthless, and the exploitative. They are unconstrained by feelings of attachment or loyalty, see life as a game, and are motivated only by a need for power and control. Lying is for them a standard form of communication, used sometimes even when it is unnecessary and conveys no apparent advantage.

Unfortunately, such people are usually glib, charming, and able to draw others to them. In fact, although they occupy as much as 4 percent of the population, they remain largely invisible to the rest of us. Many of them gravitate toward hierarchical occupations that allow them to dominate and exploit others, notably business (especially sales), politics, and the military, though they can be found anywhere. Their defining characteristic is a capacity for deceit. To be in the presence of a sociopath can be a very confusing experience. Once it begins to dawn on you that they are so self-centered that no concept such as the rights and needs of others ever crosses their mind, they begin to seem like people from another planet. Feelings that the rest of us are prone to — shame, embarrassment, and remorse — are missing.

They are impulsive and reckless, which, oddly, makes them especially attractive to those who experience their own lives as boring. Martha Stout in her book *The Sociopath Next Door* characterizes their seductive appeal as follows:

> Let us take your credit card and fly to Paris tonight. Let us take your savings and start that business that sounds so foolish but, with two minds like ours, could really take off. Let us go down to the beach and watch the hurricane. Let us get married right now. Let us lose these boring friends of yours and go off somewhere by ourselves. Let us have sex in the elevator. Let us invest your money in this hot tip I just got. Let us laugh at the rules. Let us see how fast your car can go. Let us live a little.

While typically aggressive and irritable, most of these people do not end up as serial killers. They tend instead to be small-time con men, entirely self-absorbed and incapable of love, who leave a trail of broken hearts and ruined lives in their wake. You care about these men (and 90 percent of them are men) at your own risk. To get involved with one of them is a failure of imagination that results in our accepting their lies at face value. Those of us used to living with the constraints of conscience find it hard to imagine what it is like to be shameless and operating solely on the basis of one's own perceived self-interest.

One man I was evaluating who was facing incarceration after a long criminal career described how he passed bad checks at banks. He would dress in a suit and then choose the teller who looked most vulnerable, always a woman. As he approached her, he opened his jacket to reveal handcuffs on his belt. While he never said he was a cop, thus avoiding the charge of impersonating one, the handcuffs and his professional appearance were enough that the check was usually cashed.

To call such a person dishonest is to understate their determination to take advantage of those around them. They are often highly intelligent and good at simulating emotions that they do not actually feel, such as remorse. This convincing mask is the reason why they are often able to escape the legal consequences of their behavior, particularly while they are young. Judges, social workers, and therapists, people one would expect to know better, are often deceived by the apparent earnest regret and false promises of the sociopath, and as a result the legal system often treats them with leniency until their accumulated offenses reveal their true characters. This is unfortunate because, lacking the internal restraint of conscience, sociopaths generally change their behavior only in response to external consequences.

Sometimes sociopaths hide behind façades of professional accomplishment: teachers, doctors, even therapists. A nurse at a VA hospital in Massachusetts a few years ago began killing her elderly patients with overdoses of epinephrine. When she was eventually found out and convicted, a common question asked by people who knew her was, "Why did she do it?" Her victims were strangers to her and she apparently gained nothing by their deaths. As I listened to this story, I was reminded of the tale of the rabbit and the scorpion meeting on the bank of a river. The scorpion asks the rabbit to swim him across on his back. The rabbit is understandably hesitant but the scorpion reassures him. When they reach the other side the scorpion stings him. As the rabbit is dying he says, "Why did you do that?" The scorpion responds, "It's my nature."

౩౨

The most obvious sign that one is in the presence of a highly self-absorbed person is the sense that they are not really listening to you. Having a conversation with them, one gets the impression that they are thinking about what they are going to say next rather than paying attention to what is being said to them. In an argument they tend to cling to their position and seldom change their minds in response to new facts. This trait, often evident in what passes for political discourse, is more than stubbornness. It reflects instead a commitment to one's own opinions that is impervious to both logic and to the experience of others.

People who are extremely dogmatic and opinionated often adhere to their beliefs as a way of simplifying the world and because they are fearful of uncertainty. They may also dignify their opinions as "true" simply because they see some important interest of their own at stake. While we are accustomed to paying lip service to altruism, most strongly held beliefs about how society should be organized have a tendency to be self-serving, sometimes glaringly so. It is unsurprising, for example, that the rich tend to see the world through a conservative lens and regard social welfare programs as illegitimate attempts to redistribute wealth to people who have not earned it.

On a personal level, self-absorption reveals itself in a sense of entitlement and a disregard of social rules and conventions when they conflict with one's own convenience and self-interest. The able-bodied person using handicapped parking is an example of this. Those who cheat on tests, cut in line, or lie when it is advantageous to do so — in short those who have a cynical view of what is required to succeed in life — are often simply in the habit of evaluating every situation on the basis of what is best for them. Unencumbered by a sense of obligation to others, such people may be successful, at least in the short term, which reinforces their self-centered behavior. They are not, however, great candidates for committed relationships that require give and take and an awareness of the needs of their partners.

In the presence of a self-absorbed person one has the sense that he or she lacks some important human characteristic. As I have noted, what is missing is empathy or conscience, both of which require a respect for the needs of others. Such a deficit is evident in myriad ways, but it is especially disconcerting to realize that the person you are with sees you primarily as a source of admiration. If you are willing to play this role, you are welcome in the relationship, as long as your own need to be valued does not interfere with your task of providing unqualified support and approval.

Here are some questions to ask that will illuminate these character traits: Is this person modest or arrogant? How well does he tolerate disagreement? Is she able to listen? Does he ever change his mind? Does she seem excessively vain or preoccupied with appearances? Can he laugh at himself?

Fear is the prison of the heart.

People who display traits that manifest anxiety are suffering and in search of rescue. What makes them difficult to relate to is not that they intentionally harm others; they are simply a drain on the energies of those they are close to. Their fears and insecurities place restrictions on their lives that make them self-preoccupied. When confronted with someone who is anxious, it is natural to fall back on reassurance and logic. That this doesn't usually work for long is a source of frustration to people trying to help. Anxiety is contagious; it is hard not to become nervous around someone with character traits that express a pervasive, often irrational, fear of the world and the people in it.

People who are anxious are often socially inhibited. They anticipate embarrassment and humiliation and imagine that others will judge them inadequate. They are "rejection-sensitive." All of us at times worry that others will not think well of us, will not respect us, or will not want to be our friends. People with strongly avoidant characteristics, however, so exaggerate this fear that they assume that most people are critical and disapproving. As a result, they develop a chronic shyness and a reluctance to take interpersonal risks. They will emerge from their self-protective shells only when they feel assured of uncritical acceptance, which is a lot to ask of others.

These are people who are isolated and needy. At the core of their problem is a shattered sense of self and a pervasive doubt about their own adequacy. When such a person does form a relationship, it is generally a dependent one, fraught with mistrust and fears about eventual rejection. They are guarded and it is hard to engage them in any discussion about what they are feeling. Their anticipation of rejection is often realized because of their inhibited and self-denigrating style, and so their life experience reinforces their belief that others do not want to be around them. This attitude makes them vulnerable to feelings of loneliness and depression. These are people who are easily bullied when young, which confirms their belief in their own inadequacy and the malign intent of others.

Because they are painfully shy and unrealistically self-critical, such people appear to some generous souls to provide a welcome contrast to the general run of self-absorbed narcissists. It is tempting to imagine that one can provide a "corrective emotional experience." Surely anxiety about oneself will respond to caring and support, enabling the anxious person to learn to trust others and become more socially adept. But those who take on the task of saving such people in the hope that they can make them aware of their own strengths and instill feelings of self-confidence are in for a difficult time. Feelings of personal inadequacy and mistrust of others are generally not subject to modification by logic since they were not placed there by logic in the first place. To imagine that one can "teach" someone to become a different person makes for good theater (*My Fair Lady*) but more often ends in frustration and failure. Trying to love someone who does not love himself is generally a disappointing experience.

Anxiety can also be expressed in what is called the dependent style. Here we have people whose primary need is to be taken care of. Nearly all of us have a desire to be at the center of someone's life. What separates us from those who manifest a clinging dependency is a matter of degree; most of us retain a capacity to care for ourselves that allows us to function autonomously, to be alone. Those who cannot manage this have trouble making decisions; they require constant reassurance from others. In return they are self-sacrificing to a fault. They are prepared to tolerate all manner of mistreatment, emotional and physical. They are overrepresented among the ranks of abused wives, willing to endure unimaginable pain over long periods of time, unable to articulate for others an answer to the question, "Why don't you leave him?"

People who are dependent have difficulty making decisions, even small ones. They find it hard to stand up for themselves and are compliant and self-effacing in relationships. They do not initiate activities because of their lack of self-confidence, preferring to leave decisions about what to do to others. They fear abandonment and cling to those they see as reliable sources of strength and support.

Again we are confronted with the consequences of low self-esteem, in this case so diminished that a dependent person can only visualize existing in a relationship in which control of one's life is handed over to another. This submissiveness is highly unattractive to most people who are used to the independence and give and take that characterizes healthy relationships. Some, however, particularly those with a need to control others, actively seek out people with dependent traits. A common example of this dynamic is the dependent woman who marries a dominant man for security, then chafes at his efforts to control her when she matures into a more self-sufficient person.

And here is the paradox: Those preoccupied with a fear of abandonment often suffer it. Some of us find it flattering to have another person apparently so in love with us that they can hardly let us out of their sight, who require help with every decision, who are willing to surrender themselves to our wills, who clearly *need* us to feel secure. But not many of us have the energy and patience to live two lives simultaneously, ours and someone else's. Are you prepared to be the sole emotional refuge of another?

None of us live anxiety-free lives. To do so would mean that we were taking no chances and were entirely secure about who we are and what we are doing. Given the uncertainties that we all must cope with, we would have to depart from reality to eliminate anxiety entirely. Nevertheless, we can all recognize the disadvantages of *excessive* anxiety of the sort that causes us to worry constantly so that our lives are dominated by unrealistic fears.

Those who are in the grip of continual "free-floating" anxiety that restricts their choices and their behavior are extremely difficult to be around. In fact, a contagiousness about anxiety causes others to manifest it as well. The process of listening to someone with persistent and improbable worries is often an exercise in futile reassurance. We all have had the experience of trying to cope with a childhood terror: the monster under the bed or darkness concealing imaginary dangers. These are primitive fears that are resistant to reassurance because they symbolize larger issues of helplessness and lack of control. In fact, repeated attempts at reassurance can have the effect of *increasing* anxiety: "Why do people keep telling me that everything is okay?"

Anxiety leads to a lot of avoidance behavior. If being in crowds makes us apprehensive, avoiding situations where people gather is natural. Because this strategy works in the short term, it can lead to a pattern of withdrawal, with fewer and fewer social contacts, and in extreme cases to "agoraphobia," in which people are afraid to leave the house at all. People with phobic anxiety have specific areas of their life — flying, driving, public speaking, crossing bridges — in which they are inhibited by their fears from operating freely.

People who are excessively careful and safety conscious base their attitudes and behaviors on the apparently evidence-based reality that bad things happen unexpectedly all the time. Children are kidnapped, planes crash, cars collide, violent criminals do their work, buildings collapse in a world that is full of random catastrophe. The fact that the probability of any of these events happening to any one of us is low is outweighed by the terrible outcome and unpredictability of such occurrences.

And so for those whose lives are dominated by fear and worry, envisioning the peaceful, low-stress existence that most of us seek is very difficult. Anxiety results in a kind of hyperalertness that feeds on itself. The final stage experienced by anxiety sufferers occurs when they become anxious about being anxious. Their fears lose any attachment to reality and their withdrawal from life becomes profound. The paradox here is that excessive anticipation of disaster guarantees unhappiness rather than safety. Our lives shrink, our choices become limited, even our sleep declines. Our bodies, flooded by the adrenaline of the "fight or flight" response, suffer. As we await disaster we become hypochondriacs of the mind.

Anxious people evoke in us a desire to reassure them. Short of psychological treatment (often involving medication), however, they cannot let go of their irrational fears. They make poor company because of their preoccupations. As parents, they are at high risk to be overprotective and pass their fears to their children.

So many mistakes in our early attempts to choose whom to be with flow from a misunderstanding of how people change and the limitations that each of us face in our ability to alter the life and attitudes of another. Anxious people often generate in us the fantasy that we can with our reassurance rescue them from their fears. This idea is an evocation of a generous, though usually futile, overestimation of the power of love that ignores the formidable forces of habit and biological vulnerability that sustain maladaptive fears. We are all aware of the recurrent story of people who imagine that the object of their affections will change in fundamental ways after marriage: stop drinking, become more responsible with money, or achieve better control of their anger or anxiety.

Recognizing excessive anxiety in others is not difficult. Unrealistic fears, avoidance behaviors, and excessive worry are all obvious, even to the person who suffers them. It is true that people are capable of great changes over the course of their lives. Indeed the whole experience of psychotherapy is predicated on the capacity of patients to reach new understandings that lead to more adaptive behaviors. To assume, however, that any of us has the ability to alter well-established character traits and habitual ways of experiencing the world is likely to lead to disappointment. None of us is very good at modifying the well-established outlook and actions of another. Our attempts to do so are regularly met with frustration and resentment.

Always borrow from a pessimist;
he won't expect to be paid back.

Consider those hard-to-satisfy people who struggle with obsessive-compulsive personalities. These are the perfectionists whose fear of being out of control is expressed by a need to order the details of their lives in surprising ways. They may alphabetize the canned goods in their cupboards; they are so wrapped up in preparatory detail that it may inhibit their ability to accomplish anything; they are inflexible, judgmental, and rule-bound. People with these traits frequently make excellent students and workers, conscientious and deferential to authority. Many of them appear to prefer work to leisure. Meanwhile, they tend to drive those who are close to them crazy with their rigidity and need for control. They like things done their way. While they characteristically revert to compulsive behaviors when they are stressed, they are peculiarly vulnerable to depression since their desire for perfection can never be satisfied in a highly imperfect world.

(Don't, by the way, confuse this personality type and

so-called Obsessive-Compulsive Disorder, or OCD, which is anxiety-driven. People suffering from OCD are the checkers and hand-washers, who feel compelled to perform rituals that they recognize as meaningless or struggle to suppress unwanted thoughts or images. While those with OCD are troubled by their disorder and the restrictions that it imposes on them, those with obsessive-compulsive personality most often justify their urges in the name of maintaining a necessary orderliness in their lives.)

They are frequently pack rats, unable to dispose of old newspapers, clothes, or possessions they will never use again. They tend to be stubborn and miserly, both with money and affection. They are often overly intellectual and uncomfortable with feelings, theirs or others'. They devote a lot of time to planning, but are commonly delayed by their preoccupation with details. They are seldom satisfied and frequently given to outrage at the imperfections they encounter in the world around them. They are highly critical and tend to reserve their harshest judgments for their own failure to meet their elevated standards. They make lists and are preoccupied with "productivity." They are reluctant to take vacations, and when they do go they frequently bring work with them and remain electronically tied to the office. Traveling with them can consist of forced marches from one tourist site to the next. Sitting on a beach is "wasting time."

The paradox that pervades the lives of people with this style is that an obsessive need to control leads to a loss of control. (Hence the proverb, "The perfect is the enemy of the good.") Every violation of the rules is a crack in the façade of their vision of How Things Should Be. They are pessimists, burdened by the knowledge of how impossible it is to control everything and everyone around them. They are uniquely vulnerable to discouragement. They tend to have conservative beliefs, are frequently religious (more rules), and are uncomfortable with the "decadence" and immorality that surrounds them. The past looks better to them than the future.

Since they live with constant self-criticism, they are hard on others. They are therefore difficult to live with and usually intolerant of the disorder and fallibility that children represent. Sometimes love can cause them to make exceptions. My father, an orthopedic surgeon, was an obsessive-compulsive workaholic (would you want an easygoing surgeon?) and very judgmental. But somehow he carved out a space for my mother and me to inhabit in which love overcame perfectionism, and he was an exceptionally tolerant husband and father. When he attended my ice hockey games, however, he was much more likely to talk afterward about some detail involving the skates or sticks than he was about the outcome of the game itself.

One has to be careful in forming relationships with those who are preoccupied with order and control — unless you are especially dependent or histrionic and need help organizing your life. Then, provided that neither of you change and you develop a high tolerance for boredom, you may live happily ever after.

A group of people with similar character traits are those whose style is termed depressive. Here we have those whose characteristic view of the world is gloomy and relentlessly pessimistic. The term *depression* is commonly used to describe transient mood shifts that may be perfectly normal reactions to temporary setbacks such as rejection in love, a poor test grade, or a minor traffic accident. People with a depressive personality, however, exhibit a chronic and pervasive sense of inadequacy, futility, and self-blame. Their lives are filled with worry and they are nearly incapable of experiencing pleasure. Like those with obsessive traits, their tendency toward self-criticism is frequently turned on others and takes the form of harsh judgments about those closest to them. These are very difficult people to be around.

Because they are so self-denigrating, depressives often inspire rescue fantasies on the part of those who imagine that they can save them. Typically, a caring friend or relative will attempt, often over and over, to reassure the depressed person that "you're being too hard on yourself." The negativism and irrational guilt that are such prominent personality features are often the subject of logical arguments that point out the suffering person's strengths and fundamental worth. When these approaches prove futile, the rescuer commonly feels exasperation and anger that leads to distancing and rejection, thus confirming the depressed person's professed belief in his own worthlessness and the futility of life.

Sometimes depression, like anxiety, manifests itself as humility, which can appear to be an admirable trait in a world full of self-centered display. There is a big difference, however, between modesty and glumness. The latter drains pleasure from every moment and is crippling and contagious. To be with a glum person is inevitably a commentary on our hopes for our own lives. Are we content to brood and worry along with them? Do we imagine that we can convince them that the effort to be happy is a risk worth taking? Do we wish to accommodate their chronic feelings of guilt and regret?

The decision to draw closer to such a person and try to save them from themselves by liberal applications of sympathy and love is unlikely to succeed in the long run. The world being what it is, the pessimists among us have ample ammunition to support their gloomy outlooks. And in the end, they, like hypochondriacs, will ultimately be proven right: each life does end badly. To try to convince them that one can be happy in the face of this discouraging fact is usually an exercise in disappointment. Depressive personalities are the black holes of the psychiatric universe, traps for even the light that their well-intentioned friends try to use to lead them out of the darkness.

We live in a society that has "medicalized" human suffering. In an effort to remove the stigma from mental illness, we have redefined a lot of habitual behaviors, such as a vulnerability to alcohol, as diseases. This can lead to a belief that all sorts of mood disorders, even those embedded in our personalities, are subject to medical treatment. Such a construction ignores the reality that we are all ultimately responsible for the way we interpret the world and interact with the people in it. If we remain fixated on the most discouraging aspects of life — its apparent randomness, the frequency of heartbreak, the illusory nature of control, the inevitability of aging and death, the many ways our best hopes can be frustrated — we are going to be unhappy and a drag on those around us. Our lives may come to resemble the story of two women at lunch in the Catskills. One says, "The food in this place is terrible!" The other responds, "Yes, and they give you such small portions." From such attitudes, there is no escape. Think twice before linking your life to such a person.

꒰ꞋꞋ꒱

And then there are those described as passive-aggressive. Their negativity and discouragement are expressed indirectly by "forgetting" and slowing down. These are people who resist demands that they function at levels expected of everyone else. They demonstrate procrastination and inefficiency in completing assigned tasks. In any group undertaking they are reluctant to pull their weight. Naturally, these habits evoke a lot of resentment in those around them, especially coworkers, with resultant feelings on the part of passive-aggressive people of being unappreciated and misunderstood. Typically, they are chronic complainers, resistant and hostile to authority.

Their lack of success, both occupationally and socially, leaves them angry and aggrieved. They are pessimistic about the future and have an abiding sense that life is unfair. They are frequently sullen and argumentative, envious of the success of others, and convinced of the unfairness of life.

They also feel relatively powerless. This style, for example, is characteristic of children who are resisting parental authority. They cannot do so openly because of their relatively small physical and psychological size. What they *can* do is slow down, "forget," and perform poorly. Parents are naturally frustrated by this sort of behavior and attribute it to the child "not listening" or fully understanding what is required of them. This leads to repeated reprimands and lectures, which are ignored and only produce more resentment in the child. The cycle consists of instructions, nonperformance, anger, criticism, and more instructions. When these interactions become habitual, the danger is that passive resistance to authority may become a permanent part of the child's character — not an effective strategy for long-term success, in the workplace or with personal relationships.

Think about people of your acquaintance who are always late, habitually promise more than they deliver, and have trouble meeting their obligations. That they feel unappreciated and are resentful of those who are more successful makes them even harder to be around. Because their intentions appear good it takes awhile to discover the disparity between words and behavior. Unkept promises are more frequently the products of hostility than of absentmindedness. If you find yourself alternating between puzzlement and anger at the nonperformance of another person, think "passive-aggressive."

What is important about all these different personality types is not that they are likely to be manifested in pure, easily recognizable form. If this were true we would have little trouble identifying and avoiding them. Instead, there is a good deal of overlap between them, and all of us at one time or another manifest traits that interfere with our ability to get what we want from other people.

For example, a natural human reaction to being told what to do is to resist doing it until we receive an explanation of why we should and why the assigned task is important to us or the organization of which we are a part. Lacking such an explanation we may decide that the order is illegitimate and that our time and energy are being wasted. We then have the choice of asking for clarification of purpose. Or we may decide to put the task off, or we do it reluctantly or inefficiently as a commentary on our lack of enthusiasm. My favorite story in this regard concerns a boss who is determined to have 100 percent participation in his company's United Fund campaign. Informed that one of the workers is refusing to give, he asks to see the man. "Johnson," he says, "Let me put it this way, either you contribute or you're fired." "I'd be happy to contribute," replies the worker. Surprised, the boss asks, "Well then, why didn't you contribute before?" The worker says, "Nobody ever explained the United Fund to me before."

We can, in other words, adopt a passive-aggressive approach to work or personal responsibilities. If we do so, it is important to notice what we're doing and understand both the origins of the behavior and potential consequences. (Whoever assigned us the task we are avoiding is likely to notice.) We should also be honest with ourselves about whether this response is habitual or occasional. Our job and marriage might depend on it.

ༀ

In relationships, any of the styles discussed are likely to leave a trail of broken hearts and angry people in their wake. A primary question people ask about personality problems is this: Is the person manifesting them responsible for his or her behavior? These groupings of traits are, after all, listed in the *Diagnostic and Statistical Manual of Mental Disorders.* Are they therefore illnesses for which people are not to blame? Or do they represent choices for which each of us ought to be held accountable?

Legally, this question has been answered. Courts do not, in general, accept a diagnosis of a personality disorder as meeting the criteria for an insanity defense. Jails are full of sociopaths (those who qualify for a diagnosis of Antisocial Personality Disorder). This fact reflects a tacit assumption that people whose whole lives reflect a clear pattern of maladaptive behaviors are nevertheless legally responsible for the consequences of their actions.

Most people who suffer from personality disorders, whether diagnosed or not, do not end up in legal difficulties. Instead they burden and push away those around them who find many of their behaviors inexplicable. Unlike those with other psychological disorders (generalized anxiety, major depression, psychotic illness), people who exhibit destructive personal styles are typically unaware of and therefore untroubled, at least consciously, by the habitual patterns of thought and action that alienate them from others. People almost uniformly justify their outlooks and behaviors by imagining that their particular view of the world is accurate, whatever others may think.

This tendency toward self-justification affects us all. Deeply religious people or those with strong political beliefs, for example, frequently find it puzzling that everyone who is intelligent and well-intentioned doesn't see the world as they do. That is why so much argument and proselytizing, in what often appears to be a "dialogue of the deaf," typifies the endless philosophical and political discussions that characterize our society. Frequently absent is humility and tolerance for other views. We like to imagine ourselves as acting on the basis of conscious reason. That this is not the case is demonstrated by the ways in which we repetitively do things that are not in our self-interest. Look at the prevalence of addictions, the high divorce rate, and our eating habits.

If we can accept the truth that most of what we do is the result of unexamined routine and subconscious motives, we can begin to look at patterns of behavior, ours and others', that we might want to reconsider. First we must be convinced that what we are doing now is not adaptive. Then we must believe in the task of self-examination as a preliminary to alternative behaviors.

Are there elements of our personal styles that are not

working for us? Are we having trouble drawing close to others? Do we appear to be alienating people? Are we sabotaging our careers even though we are competent at our jobs? Are we involved in repetitively unsatisfying relationships? Affirmative answers to these sorts of questions suggest that something is going on in our lives that is beneath our level of awareness. We would do well to examine our habitual ways of interacting with others (or the natures of the people we are choosing to interact with) to help us decide what needs to be changed.

The most important factor in determining how happy we are is the quality of our interpersonal relationships. We differ in the number of other people to whom we are attached. Few of us, however, are equipped to spend our lives alone. It is no accident that the most feared punishment for those in prison is solitary confinement. Even people already denied most of the comforts of everyday freedom cannot long abide isolation. Of all the psychic pain that human beings suffer, loneliness is for most the worst. Being ignored is the final insult to our humanity. The perpetrators of mass murder are customarily found to be people who feel the sting of being forsaken by a world they cannot join.

Few of us get through life without experiencing rejection. How we respond to it, how we soothe ourselves, and how we gain the acceptance we need from those we admire, determine the lives we will lead. Talent, resolve, luck, genes, the accident of birth, all play a role in the kind of people we become. But the ability to attach meaning to our existence depends more than anything else on those traits, inborn and acquired, that affect our ability to relate to others on whom our happiness depends. From our earliest days upon the earth we are surrounded and sustained by a web of relationships, ever-changing and in need of constant maintenance. Without this network, untethered, we cannot survive emotionally. This is why we must choose those to whom we are connected with infinite care and for the right reasons. If the web breaks, we have a long way to fall.

To be in the presence of a depressed person is an exercise in discouragement. Terms like *pessimism* and *hopelessness* describe the attitude of people who believe things will turn our badly and who often take a kind of perverse satisfaction when their expectations are met. They have a cynical outlook and a contempt for those who dare to hope. They are suspicious of people's motives and express a pervasive mistrust of others. They are given to generalizations: "All politicians are crooked." "Trust no one." "If I didn't have bad luck, I'd have no luck at all." They tend to hold strong prejudices against whole categories of people. The world is a dangerous and bleak place . . . and getting worse.

Anyone who has spent time watching people in public places can learn to recognize depression in the faces of passers-by. This is not an infallible diagnostic tool, especially in the young. (Lincoln is supposed to have said, "We're all responsible for our faces after 40.") Before time has had a chance to permanently alter our expressions, before the corners of our mouths turn down in a mask of sadness and regret, people can disguise their discouragement and cynicism in an effort to avoid alienating others. As is the case in deciphering any habitual attitude, therefore, one needs to listen to what people say and observe what they do.

What we are looking for are those who are judgmental, expect (and often evoke) hostility and incompetence in others, believe they are the only good driver on the road, are sure that airline personnel are there to lie to customers, expect that dropped toast will inevitably hit the carpet jam side down.

A devastated sense of self is another clue that one is in the presence of a depressed person. The belief that one is unworthy or inadequate can be disguised by a cynical façade and by criticism of others, but a depressed outlook has at its core a sense that the world is a reflection of our inner despair and an anticipation that most human enterprises, including relationships, end badly. Such anticipation has a way of becoming self-fulfilling. These are difficult people to be around because many of them suffer what is formally called *anhedonia,* an inability to experience pleasure. This quality makes them the death of any party (or any relationship) they might participate in.

A formal diagnosis of depression requires certain criteria, including appetite disturbance, sleep problems, fatigue, low self-esteem, indecisiveness, and hopelessness. People with depressive personalities may manifest some or all of these characteristics some or all the time. More important is the overall affect that they habitually display, a moroseness and discouragement that makes it impossible for them to experience sustained joy and tends to discourage the people around them. If you are trying to relate to such a person, you will likely find your own mood shifting in the direction of depression.

In an effort to explain how we feel, we usually try to establish a cause and effect relationship between external events and inner feelings. Those with depressed personalities, however, experience situations and people independent of actual events. Like all those whose attitudes are driven by maladaptive long-term beliefs about how the world works, they do not have a satisfactory explanation for their chronic discouragement. What they really seek is confirmation for their pessimism and someone to share it. You do not want to be this sharing person, no matter how compassionate you are or how powerful you imagine your love can be.

No hell is private.

We are defined by whom and what we love. No single set of personality traits is associated with substance abuse. While it is true that people who are prone to addiction commonly manifest impulsivity, recklessness, a tendency toward depression, and difficulties sustaining relationships, by the time one is identified as a substance abuser the secondary consequences of alcoholism or drug use are so life altering that one's underlying personality structure is difficult to apprehend.

A great source of confusion is that the use of alcohol is a legal, socially sanctioned activity indulged in harmlessly by most members of society. Prescription drugs with mood altering potential and a capacity for abuse and dependency are also widely used. We are inundated by advertising that suggests that we need not tolerate physical or emotional discomfort when such medicines are available. It is hardly surprising, then, that people with a biological vulnerability to addictions are going to get into trouble with both legal and illegal substances.

While this predisposition cannot be reliably predicted (though it tends to run in families), once it begins to man-

ifest itself in adolescence there are a variety of danger signals. The most obvious may be some ancillary form of
addiction such as an eating disorder, which, after all, is an
inability to rationally manage one's relationship with a
substance, in this case, food. The indications that one is
going to have a long-term problem with alcohol or drugs
appear during early exposure. Not all who drink to excess
in high school or college are going to end up alcoholic,
but such behavior while young is not a hopeful sign. A
good rule for alerting oneself to a potential for substance
abuse is that *if you think there might be a problem, there probably is.* People tend to deny or underreport their alcohol
consumption, and it falls to those who care about them,
particularly family members, to give a more honest evaluation. Sometimes this concern may progress to a form
of confrontation by friends and family — an intervention
— to persuade the substance abuser to seek help, defined
as a formal treatment program with the goal of absti-
nence. Anything short of this for a confirmed addict is a
fantasy. Even the best of these programs have relapse
rates in excess of 70 percent, which gives you a sense of
what you are taking on to knowingly link your life to that
of a substance abuser.

One way of thinking about personality disorders is to
see them as bad habits, well established patterns of be-

havior that are virtually automatic and distinctive parts of our character structures. They are deeply ingrained traits that, taken together, express who we are. In this sense, our dependence on substances — drugs, alcohol, food, nicotine — are commentaries on how we see ourselves. Even "constructive addictions," to exercise or collecting things, for example, can pose their own dangers. That said, the immoderate use of drugs and alcohol represent the most obvious self-inflicted threats to our psychological well-being and that of the people around us.

As with any set of ominous personality characteristics, an inability to manage drinking or drug use should be taken as a warning. Given the denial that is a hallmark of addiction, to rely on anyone's self-evaluation of their use of intoxicating substances is foolish. This is not simply because lying to others is a common characteristic of addicts. It is the lying they do to themselves that is ultimately fatal. "I can stop anytime I want," "I'm not drinking more than the people around me," and "I've never missed a day of work" are all rationalizations that alcoholics and drug addicts routinely deploy and often believe. You have to trust your own observations and instincts here to assess whether this person has a future ahead of them that you won't want to share.

It's amazing how much substance abuse, especially if it

takes the legal form of alcohol consumption, people are prepared to accept in others. It is also difficult to know, especially when we are young, how much of anything is too much, for ourselves as well as for those around us. One clue is a recurring feeling of invisibility when your significant other is drinking.

When we care about someone, we want to help, not reject, them — especially if they suffer what is nearly universally accepted as a disease. What kind of person turns his back on a sick human being? Here is the trap. Those of us who pride ourselves in our ability to care for others are susceptible to rescue fantasies that allow us to believe that "If I love this person enough, their insecurities and need for drink or drugs will evaporate." Many are the marriages that have foundered on this daydream. Some of my most difficult moments as a therapist have occurred when the spouse or parent or child of a substance abuser was forced to the shattering conclusion that their addict loved the substance he abused more than anyone or anything else in his life, including the people who loved *him* the most. If you have a choice, you do not want to face such a moment.

*Against boredom
the gods themselves fight in vain.*

A group of people to be wary of do not fit into any specific category of personality disorder. They do not, in general, seek to manipulate or disadvantage others. They are not necessarily self-absorbed or unkind, and their intentions are usually benign. And yet they are hard to be around for long. They are seldom insightful or reflective, though they may be intelligent and capable of useful work. They tend toward a certain loquaciousness and are not often good listeners. The quality of their thoughts combined with an irresistible need to communicate them are defining characteristics. They are fools.

As we pass through life, experiencing success and failure, acceptance and rejection, each of us is trying to apprehend how the world really works. Everything that happens to us, everything we know or believe, is integrated into this perception and has some effect on our subsequent behavior. Intolerance in areas of ethics, politics, or religion is the hallmark of fools. In its worst manifestations it may lead to violence against others who hold alternative beliefs.

Other examples of imperfect understanding are people who carry around misconceptions of what works and what doesn't in any important area of their lives. If one imagines, for example, that a conspiracy exists on the part of modern medicine to ignore the benefits of herbal supplements and "natural" cures, one is prone to making decisions about one's health that do not comport with scientific evidence. In its most benign form this can result in the consumption of all manner of substances with no health benefits. It can also lead to a desperate and futile pursuit of expensive and unproven remedies for serious illnesses like cancer. Similarly, the decision of some parents to not immunize their children against common childhood diseases because of an unfounded fear of vaccines endangers their kids and places us all at risk for the return of illnesses previously on their way to extinction.

Since foolishness depends on context and represents deviance from some social norm, it is not necessarily a permanent affliction. We are all familiar with the person who is an outcast in high school but a major success in later life. The deficits that define a fool — a lack of understanding, judgment, or common sense — are also remediable by experience and learning. Nevertheless, an established inability, even as a teenager, to think clearly makes one a poor candidate for a lasting relationship. People with unconventional beliefs, for example, UFO spotters or conspiracy theorists, tend to cluster together for mutual support. Membership in such groups is often a signal that one is in the presence of someone given to alternative and marginal views of how the world works.

The important component of true foolishness is a contempt or lack of understanding for the scientific method as a means of explicating the world, combined with a belief in miracles that is simply an exercise of faith. The capacity to think clearly about one's life experience is a crucial component of a successful life. If one believes that human affairs are governed by an alignment of the stars and that one's fate is determined by one's date and time of birth, one is prone to decision making that is not based on reality.

Our brains can entertain a limited number of ideas simultaneously. If our consciousness is cluttered by beliefs in magic, ghosts, paranormal phenomena, alien abduction, or the conviction that we are influenced by past lives, it is difficult to consider the variables that actually affect us.

There is a school of thought that truth is a flexible construct, elusive and subject to interpretation. In at least one area this is demonstrably not the case. Nature and its laws are intolerant of fools. When Timothy Treadwell chose to live among the Alaskan grizzlies for extended periods, he imagined that they reciprocated the affection and respect that he felt for them. He even gave them names. It turned out that while he was indulging his naïve delusions about these wild creatures they had also given him a name. That name was "food" and his life was ended by a hungry bear. Timothy was a friendly, well-meaning person, eager to talk endlessly into a video camera in an effort to educate others about these animals. The saddest part of his story is that he persuaded a young woman to accompany him on his last trip to live among them. She was also killed.

A hallmark of foolishness is an inability to learn from experience. A traditional definition of insanity applies here: doing the same things and expecting different results. All of us crave approval from others, especially our contemporaries. An important component of social learning is figuring out how to gain the acceptance and respect of those who surround us. Since none of us as children is issued an instruction manual, we discover what works socially primarily by trial and error and by treating others in the way that we would like to be treated. If we have experienced the love and approval of our parents, we are likely to have a solid sense of ourselves as valuable people and are apt to approach others with an expectation of being liked.

If, on the other hand, we have early childhood experiences of neglect or rejection, we are likely to anticipate more of the same from the people we encounter outside our families. This attitude of mistrust causes us to be vulnerable to fears of humiliation and a self-consciousness that makes it difficult to be optimistic about the outcome of new relationships. The natural defense for such fears is some form of shyness or social withdrawal that frequently results in an inability to feel comfortable with other people and an unwillingness to take the risks necessary to draw close to them. Such aloofness can also lead to scapegoating or other forms of rebuff by others. We are all aware of how cruel and exclusionary certain groups can be in adolescence. Few of us have not felt the sting of rejection.

Often mistaken for stupidity, foolishness can be the province of highly intelligent people. Recently, a past recipient of the Nobel Prize revealed sentiments about racial differences that were widely condemned and caused him to lose his job. Hearing opinions from public people (usually in areas outside their expertise) that are demonstrably absurd is common. When a U.S. senator described the internet as "a series of tubes," this was deeply revealing about his grasp of the world.

Perhaps we would do well to admit that we are all subject to superstitions, misconceptions, and delusional ideas and so are capable of acting like fools at times. As with any human failing, foolishness is a matter of degree. Still, it is sobering to imagine spending any considerable portion of one's life in the company of a judgmental, bloviating, talkative fool who is unable to profit from experience and whose opinions are not reality-based. If you seek examples of this personality type, you need only spend a little time watching the opinionated blather that passes for cable television commentary on current events. Our primary defense against such people, the remote control, is ineffective if we happen to live with them.

The best of compasses
does not point to true north.

We are, in general, unaccustomed to examining our most fundamental beliefs about the world and the people in it. Much is made of our demonstrated lack of knowledge about things that one would imagine would be basic and shared information. Whenever people are quizzed about elementary scientific facts (such as the nature of the solar system or the chemical basis of life), simple geography, or the political arrangement we live under, the results are frequently and sometimes hilariously inaccurate. Twenty percent of a recent cross-section of adult Americans were unable to locate the United States on a map of the world.

It should not be surprising then that our assumptions about people — what they want and why they behave as they do — would also be varied and based on questionable beliefs derived from an inadequate educational system, our own anecdotal experience, or the social mythology of our parents. To take one important example, do you believe that people are basically good, inclined to fairness and generosity, or are they born selfish and socialized only by the application of limit-setting and punishment? How you answer this question illuminates what you expect from others.

This might be called the Anne Frank assumption. Even as she hid with her family from people who would eventually kill her she wrote in her diary, "In spite of everything, I still believe that people are basically good at heart." As she was to discover, many people are capable of actions that contradict such a naïve generalization. Some, in fact, are prepared to fly planes into buildings with the intent to kill large numbers of those with different beliefs.

On the other hand, many are willing to help and even sacrifice themselves on behalf of others. So the truth about human motivation again turns out to be situational and a matter of emphasis. The real question becomes how to make realistic assessments of others that encourage generosity but protect us (insofar as possible) from disappointment, even malice.

Most of our disagreements about the fundamental nature of mankind play out in less dramatic fashion but are important in how we treat other people and what we expect from them. Such assumptions also play a big role in how we raise children and with what political philosophy we choose to govern ourselves. At a strictly personal level, our expectations of others determine both our personalities and our morality, our sense of right and wrong.

If, for example, we believe that we live in a world where resources are limited and only the fittest survive and propagate, we are likely to behave differently than if we believe that it is a moral goal of civilization to care for the weak even when it is not immediately in our self-interest to do so. Every interaction we have with another person is informed by our basic assumptions about what we value and believe in. And whether these behaviors persist and become habitual depends on whether we feel ourselves rewarded for them.

*We cannot direct the wind
but we can trim the sails.*

Nothing is more important than our capacity to understand how the world works and to develop adaptive behaviors that enable us to get what we need and want. In some sense this is the very definition of learning. The entire edifice of scientific thought is constructed on the premise that through the use of the experimental method we can understand the laws of nature and use this knowledge to our benefit. To cite an obvious example, in the ancient world diseases were believed to result from imbalances of bodily humors or to derive from miasmas or vengeful gods. Subsequent experimentation produced the germ theory of illness and we have arrived at a comprehension of the role of bacteria and viruses as causal agents of infectious disease.

Our understanding of why people behave as they do has lagged behind our concepts of physical disorders. We can describe our brains anatomically as collections of neurons and we can even identify the functions associated with specific areas of the brain, but why certain so-called "motivated behaviors" (hunger, sexual longing, drug-seeking behavior, or a lust for power, for example) are manifested differently in different people remains a mystery. We can see that alcoholism and anxiety run in families, but the specific biological or neurochemical basis for these disorders remains obscure.

In the present incomplete state of our knowledge about the causation of atypical behaviors we are left with a diagnostic manual of mental disorders that is essentially descriptive. If we cannot yet answer the question "why?" we can still discern patterns of behavioral symptoms that are recognizable and stable over time. This knowledge, I would argue, is useful in navigating through life, and the fact that it is not widely disseminated results in many preventable mistakes in deciding whom we can trust.

People with serious mental illness — schizophrenia, bipolar disorder, major depression — are generally so affected by their symptoms (for example, hallucinations, paranoia, manic behavior, debilitating sadness) that there is no mistaking their distress. They generally require medication, and people around them are aware that they have a profound organic illness. Those with so-called personality disorders, however, are frequently undiagnosed and may be unaware that anything in their behavior is abnormal. In fact, they frequently believe that their interpersonal difficulties are the fault of others or of society as a whole. This idea undermines people's motivation to change even when it is obvious that their lives are not working in some important respect.

These are the people we need to be able to recognize in our efforts to find happiness in the company of others. To the degree that we can discern the signals that we are in the presence of those with character difficulties we can protect ourselves from being taken advantage of by them physically, financially, or emotionally. This assumes that we have learned how to avoid *becoming* like them so that we might fulfill the traditional injunction against being either victims or exploiters, neither predators nor prey. What we are striving for instead are relationships that provide both parties with a sense of a symmetrical commitment to satisfying lives and are based on the capitalistic idea of complementarity, that in the pursuit of our self-interest we can all prosper together.

Even as we dedicate ourselves to this task, we are confronted by the fact that many people see life as a zero-sum game in which competition is primary, where opportunities for success are limited, and in which we get what we want at the expense of others. This is a widely held belief, encouraged by pyramidal corporate structures and the worlds of entertainment and sports, with their limited opportunities for success. Not all of us are going to be obscenely wealthy or featured on the pages of *US Weekly*. The inequality of economic success in the United States (where the richest 10 percent of the population controls 70 percent of the wealth) creates a class system that is discouraging to many who believe that they have failed to achieve the American dream.

There is also a widespread belief that how one does in life is determined by a variety of things over which we have little or no control: the families we are born into, the color of our skin, educational opportunities or lack thereof, and luck. These disparities produce cynicism and a sense of unfairness, not to mention crime. We are also subject to a kind of social resentment that creates a pervasive envy and discontent that results from a feeling that the system under which we operate is unfair. The social compact between rich and poor is fragile and given to breaking down in response to emergencies such as power outages or natural disasters that illuminate the disparities in wealth that we have learned to take for granted.

Against this social background, each of us struggles to define our place in the world, knowing that the rules that govern society are imperfectly enforced in a way that gives a tremendous advantage to those already privileged. It is difficult to know how this chronic sense of unfairness affects the kind of people we become and the ways in which we relate to each other. Although the subject of this book is individual happiness and how best to pursue it, it is worth reflecting on the context in which this pursuit takes place. In the effort to satisfy our own self-interest, we can choose behavior that is exploitative or we can adopt a more generous way of relating to other people. This is the choice that defines character, which is to say our habitual way of interacting with others. What is important is being able to discern those personal traits that wear well over time.

*Life is rarely as simple
as we would have it.*

One of the things that blocks our efforts to learn about the world and the people in it is the nature of the stories we are told, come to believe, and then tell others about how things work. This shared mythology, if it is incorrect, interferes with our efforts to understand ourselves and others and ultimately leads to bad decisions in the same way as explorers attempting to find their way with inadequate maps.

The opposite of truth is not necessarily the lie. It can also be another form of dishonesty, namely *sentimentality.* This takes the form of a mawkish oversimplification of the world in which reality is entirely lost. The most trivial form of this tendency can be discerned in the funeral eulogy. Gone is the actual person with his strengths and flaws. He is replaced by a paragon of wit and virtue almost unrecognizable to those who knew him best. What happens to the stories of drunks and wife beaters when they die? They make no appearance on the obituary pages. Nothing, it is said, improves one's reputation more than death.

If our descent into sentimentality were confined to well-intentioned words of comfort to the bereaved, we could be forgiven. Unfortunately, this particular form of distortion is much more widespread and consequential. In fact, our whole self-help-through-consumption, advertising culture is one long appeal to a sentimental view of the world in which we are just one purchase away from having the life we want. Don't those attractive young people with their new trucks and cold beers look happy? Could life get any better than that? Don't you enjoy those commercials that emphasize how relatively old, fat, and friendless most of us are?

In a recent poll, 81 percent of Americans said that they regularly talk to God. (It is interesting that if someone reports that God is talking to them, they are either seen as prophets or risk involuntary hospitalization.) Whatever comfort people derive from their faith and however much good is done in the name of one religion or another, the ultimate questions — Why are we here? What constitutes a moral life? What happens to us when we die? — are answered by most people by reference to archaic texts containing often contradictory stories that differ from one culture to another. No evidence of the sort that we are accustomed to demanding in other areas of our lives is required to support the truth of any element of faith; we simply believe it. In return we are given the hope provided by prayer and the assurance of immortality, no small gift in a world preoccupied with the fear of death.

Another arena in which sentimentality holds sway is politics. In choosing people to lead us through perilous times, we too frequently depend on those who divide the world along the stark lines of good and evil, us and them, and who promise to protect us against economic turbulence and terrorists who seek to destroy us. All of us would like to believe that there exist figures so powerful and wise that we can depend on them to care for us. The fact that these people, once elected, almost invariably disappoint us only makes us vulnerable to the next candidate who promises to do better. The cycle of dependency, credulity, and disillusionment plays out again and again without our learning much from it or developing a real skepticism about the sentimental stories that successive generations of politicians use to get elected. Certainly personal and philosophical differences exist between candidates. But we wait in vain for the messiah who will lead us out of the wilderness of confusion and insecurity in which we find ourselves. Such a longing can only beget disappointment.

If you want to know whether someone is telling you a sentimental story, ask yourself, "Does this sound oversimplified? Is he talking as if there were only two alternatives (such as victory or humiliation) to solving this problem?" If life teaches us anything, it is that it's complicated with many possible outcomes, only a few of which we control. If you feel like you're hearing a children's story in which the characters are cartoon depictions instead of real people, run for your life.

In our efforts to create satisfying and lasting relationships, we are at great risk of disillusionment if we imagine that *any* relationship is going to resemble the sentimental and idealized portrayals we see on our movie and television screens. The ambiguity and discernment required by the process of investing our love in someone who will reciprocate and whom we can depend on over time is a long way from the instant attractions and "happily ever after" outcomes that constitute the Hollywood version of reality. The false images of what constitutes a real and satisfying relationship are a source of great confusion to many people who are apt to oscillate between naïveté and cynicism as they search for a model of human connectedness that is realistic.

Childhood is the only time that a sentimental outlook is adaptive. Most fairy tales, with their simplified characters and morals, are comforting. As we become more aware of life's complexity, however, we need to relinquish the reassurance implied in the magical triumph of all that is good. If we do not make this transition, we are asking for a lifetime of disenchantment as adults.

Another pervasive form of sentimentality is nostalgia. It seems that everyone is old enough to remember a better time, when the world was safer, everyone was kinder, children were more respectful, and more people looked like us. What happened to that time? Where is Norman Rockwell when we need him? An astonishing number of citizens cling to a belief that we need a return to a fantasized past to reclaim the values that made this country great.

If we are ever to understand the world we live in and the people who inhabit it, we must develop a capacity for separating truth from sentimentality. We need to employ the same discrimination that we attempt to use in our financial lives, namely an ability to discern value and a healthy skepticism of those whose job it is to defraud us.

We must learn to accept the ambiguity, imperfections, and uncertainty that characterize real life while avoiding the oversimplification that is the hallmark of sentimentality. We must, in other words, learn to distinguish reality from illusion if we are to make good decisions about how to live and especially about whom to live with. Our happiness depends on the quality of these choices.

We flatter ourselves if we believe that our character is fixed.

None of our behaviors occur in a vacuum. The kind of people we are is to a significant extent determined by the situations in which we operate: the environments we are in and the people we choose to be around. We would like to think of ourselves as independent with fixed sets of values that reliably determine our actions. Plenty of evidence shows that this is not the case. Stanley Milgram in his experiments with members of the New Haven community in the 1960s demonstrated that ordinary people could be induced to inflict what they believed to be painful electric shocks on others if they thought they were participating in a learning experiment sanctioned by Yale University. All it took was someone in a white coat telling them that they must continue, even when they believed that the shocks they were administering might be life threatening. Anyone who thinks that they would not do likewise is encouraged to read Milgram's book, *Obedience to Authority*.

We have been witness to the horrors of the Holocaust, the massacre of Vietnamese civilians at My Lai, the abuse of Iraqis at Abu Ghraib, all atrocities inflicted by ordinary people that can be understood only in the contexts of time and place. The inescapable conclusion is that a capacity for both good and evil resides within each of us and is subject to situational influence. The importance of placing ourselves in circumstances and around people who are likely to bring out the best in us cannot, therefore, be exaggerated. This fact is frequently lost in the emphasis placed on personal responsibility, as if our sense of morality can reliably override any situation in which we find ourselves.

In the more mundane circumstances of our daily lives, it is clear that the kinds of people we choose to surround ourselves with have a big influence on the way we behave. The phenomenon of peer pressure for teenagers is well established and the cliques that we belong to (or are excluded from) in high school say a lot about the kinds of people we are and become. Every parent's apprehension about his or her child's development is either diminished or accelerated by the people their child chooses as friends. Those primarily interested in academics, for example, tend to hang together, as do those for whom drug use is the center of their social lives. There is certainly some overlap in categories, but on the whole we prefer to be around those in whom we can see some reflection of ourselves.

An important component of our effort to become the person we want to be is to carefully choose the people with whom we spend time. In making these choices we are doing more than selecting others who like to do the same things we do. We are also making a statement about what values and personality traits we wish to nurture. Every significant relationship we have in our lives changes us. In many ways we become like those who are important to us. Who has not been surprised when their behavior or feelings unexpectedly remind them of a parent? "I'm becoming more like my father as I get older" is a frequent and rueful acknowledgement of this influence.

And so it is to a greater or lesser extent with everyone we have been close to in our lives. This is why we need to choose our friends carefully. They and what they value will affect us far into the future.

When we begin to experiment with intimacy, our first loves are usually drawn from whatever group we have become a part of. How we interact is affected by the social mores and philosophical beliefs of the group. By this time the outline of our personalities is already clear and is either changed or reinforced by the people to whom we choose to draw close. A lot of this adjustment is taking place at a level below our consciousness, which leads us to believe that what we identify as love is a mysterious process that cannot be analyzed or understood fully. We observe that shared interests play some role in our choice of those with whom we will be intimate, but we are in general content to indulge the inscrutability of the process that draws us to one person above all others.

Usually, no one has explained to us in any systematic way the concept of personality styles, the collection of traits that each of us manifest. So we are flying blind, powered by hormonal drives and superficial concepts of attractiveness defined by the larger culture but with no real understanding of how to predict how people will behave or how they (and we) will change in the future. Unfortunately, we have only a few years of this uninformed experimentation before we are expected to begin to make permanent decisions about whom we expect to live with, have children with, and grow old with. One would expect a significantly high error rate in such a process and the frequency of divorce affirms that such is the case. In some ways it's a miracle that *any* of these decisions work out well.

We would do well to consider the role of context in our lives so that while we are paying attention to the kinds of people with whom we spend our time we also weigh the places and situations that constitute our surroundings. I have heard many people wonder why so many of their friends appear to have drinking problems when it turns out that the locus of much of their social life is in bars. There is no behavior that does not have an effect, however small, on our self-esteem. Everything we do, every place we visit, every person we interact with has some impact on our sense of ourselves. Once again, folk wisdom comes to our aid: "Lie down with dogs; get up with fleas" or, more optimistically, "An eagle does not catch flies." These cautions are especially important insofar as our choices of people and places become habitual and thereby an expression of who we are.

What is essential
is invisible to the eye.

Perhaps the best advice that can be given in teaching people how to evaluate relationships is to take your time. Most of us are given to making decisions rapidly and basing them on insufficient evidence. Many of our purchases, for example, are what retailers like to call "impulse buys," which is why much effort is expended by those who sell things on the science of packaging and something called product placement. An article of faith for the advertising industry is that people make decisions on what to purchase based on the most superficial considerations. You may be sure that a great deal of thought was given to the title and cover design of this book. And as much effort was lavished on the external features of the car you drive as went into the engine that propels it. While we all believe ourselves competent to judge appearances, few of us are expert mechanics.

And so in a sense we are conditioned to pay unwarranted attention to surface attributes when making decisions about what to buy. That this tendency affects our social judgments can be seen most clearly in our entertainment culture. Who occupies our interest? Who inhabits the pages of our magazines? Whom do we wish we looked like? When I think of the people I interned with at a large teaching hospital, I am struck by how little they resembled the staff on *Grey's Anatomy*. (Nor, unfortunately, did any of us have nearly as much sex in nearly as many places as the housestaff of Seattle Grace.) Apart from creating a kind of chronic dissatisfaction with ourselves, this phenomenon also causes us to place excessive value on superficial characteristics in evaluating others.

Choosing a friend, which is or should be the first stage in forming any relationship, is a little like buying a used car. Everyone we meet has a certain quantity and quality of "mileage" that they have accumulated. This is their life story, and it takes awhile to get it from someone we have just met. We each carry around different versions of our pasts that sometimes bear only a loose resemblance to what has actually happened to us. This is because our memories are not perfect recorders and because the interpretations we place on our experiences vary with the image of ourselves that we are trying to portray. The story also tends to change with the person we are telling it to.

As a therapist, for example, I am used to hearing versions of people's lives that they may not have shared with others, even those they are closest to.

It is therefore important for each of us to realize that what we are hearing from people talking about themselves is an expurgated account of their pasts that customarily exaggerates traits or accomplishments that the person telling the story imagines will be valued by the listener. How accurate the information is can sometimes be determined only by talking to others who were there. I frequently commiserate with people going through divorce who wish they had taken the opportunity for some premarital conversation with their spouse's ex-partners.

Even if we are reasonably certain that we have an accurate account of someone's past, knowing what to make of it is still a challenge. We definitely have trouble predicting what anyone will do or be like in a day or a year, much less a decade. There are obvious red flags. Those who correspond with prison inmates in the hope of romance are, in general, at high risk of disappointment. The same might be said of those who look for love in bars, though many people do, sometimes with happy outcomes.

More important than where you meet someone is your ability to evaluate his or her character. Where, for example, are we to learn the signs that indicate that the person we are talking to is primarily attuned to the beating of his own heart? When does an appealing flirtatiousness signal a shallowness of thought and emotion? What is the difference between spontaneity and impulsivity? How well-organized does one have to be before a need for control becomes disagreeable? These and questions like them need to be asked about everyone with whom we are contemplating friendship. They speak to issues like integrity, reliability, and above all, compatibility. Because, whether we realize it or not, our searches for the beloved other depend on what reflections of ourselves we see when we look into their eyes.

This is the unspoken reality of our most intimate relationships and the reason behind the often unhappy truth that *we nearly always get the spouses we deserve.* It is also, incidentally, the force behind the bitterness of most divorces: We are engaged in an effort to exorcise our own least admired characteristics.

To concentrate for the moment on the selection process, we are trying to simultaneously evaluate the person in front of us (for example, where is the line between a social drinker and a drunk?) and make some guesses about what this person will be like when her skin is wrinkled. Here is where our ability to pay attention and discern behavioral patterns becomes important. Our capacity to extrapolate into the future is also relevant. If we listen closely to what therapists call (redundantly) "the past history," this may not be as difficult as you might imagine. And, as previously noted, our basic personalities are remarkably stable over time.

This process of getting to know someone involves a lot of conversation, but it must also include observations of how they behave under different circumstances. How do they treat others, especially those who are providing a service? What are their friends like? What sort of temper do they display? How do they manage frustration? What kind of driver are they? What is their relationship to money? We are trying, in other words, to discern our prospective friend's philosophy of life to decide how compatible it is with our own. If we value kindness over cruelty, compatibility over competition, generosity over parsimony, we need to see how this person behaves in a variety of situations. Hence the importance of time in getting to know someone.

The first duty of love
is to listen.

No single characteristic reveals as much about a person as their ability to pay attention to others. We live in a culture in which most people feel silenced. The voices emanating from our radios and televisions are often loud, opinionated, and relatively few in number, though the advent of Internet blogging has changed this somewhat. Our educational system gives weight to the knowledge and opinions of those who are older (but not too old) and designated as authorities. Our political leadership routinely presents us with self-serving lies and rationalizations. Most people never imagine being able to gain access to the public megaphone or have anyone outside their immediate social circle pay the slightest attention to what they say or believe. And even among those closest to us, a capacity for listening is typically not well developed. We are, in general, starved for attention.

In my work as a therapist, I wish I could say that people benefit most from the wisdom and blinding insights that I bring to the process. Truthfully, most of what I do is sit in silence and try to formulate questions that will assist patients to figure out what they should do to change their lives. To do this I must pay close attention to what they are saying. Why would people spend money to engage in such a process with another human being whose own life may be no happier or more fulfilling than their own? The answer, of course, is that most people find it beneficial to be listened to nonjudgmentally by a societally designated healer. Many benefit equally from similar (and less expensive) interactions with their hairdresser, bartender, or clergyman.

To be able to focus on the expressed needs and desires of another person, especially when you are not being paid for it, reflects a generosity of spirit that is not randomly distributed in the population. Such attention conveys a respect for the person being listened to that is unmistakable and satisfies our deepest human longing for connectedness. If it is true that we enter and leave this world alone, few of us can live that way for very long without going mad.

Little wonder then that we crave the experience of being heard and respond gratefully to anyone who will do this for us. We are aware at some level that the ability to listen is highly correlated with other desirable traits such as kindness, unselfishness, and empathy. The opposite is also true: It has been said of one of our most famous and opinionated television commentators that talking with him is like trying to drink from a fire hose.

The implications for a deficit in listening skills are ominous. The most obvious characteristic of people who are unable to attend to others is a lack of interest in what the other person is saying. To really listen to another is more than good manners; it is an affirmation that the person who is speaking has something to teach us.

Like any desirable human characteristic, an aptitude for listening can be faked. Those who make their living by deceiving others, unscrupulous salespeople for example, are frequently superficially charming with a practiced ability to project an interest that they do not feel. Their motto: Always be sincere, whether you mean it or not. It can be difficult to determine whether one is in the presence of such a person, though if the transaction involves money or sex, we need to be cautious. In the end, this distinction can only be made over time, another argument against the sentimental mythology of "love at first sight."

When all is said and done,
more is said than done.

A part from an inability or unwillingness to listen, other behaviors should alert us to the fact that we are in the presence of a controlling, exploitative, or self-centered person. In any list of desirable traits, *reliability* ranks high. People who consistently do what they promise to do are surprisingly uncommon. This reflects the New Year's resolution phenomenon: We all know what we *should* do to become the people we would like to be. Unfortunately, we are so used to breaking promises to ourselves that it becomes a habit that accounts for the lies, unconscious or deliberate, that we tell others. "I'll call you tomorrow," is frequently more a way of extricating oneself from the present moment than a statement of actual intent.

Chronic lateness or forgetfulness usually signifies an unappealing tendency toward passive-aggressive behavior rather than a sign that a person is busy, preoccupied, or needs a louder alarm clock. Any unkept promise ought to be interpreted as a statement of priorities. Usually, we are expected to consider such oversights as accidental and therefore no one's fault. If they constitute a pattern of behavior, however, we ignore them at our own risk.

How we feel when in the presence of another person is an excellent indicator of the value of the relationship. As I mentioned, every human interaction makes us feel a little better or worse about ourselves. Sometimes the difference is large. If we save someone's life we have a right to feel heroic. If we allow someone to merge on the freeway, we improve for a moment our sense of ourselves. Conversely, if we cut them off, we are likely to lose some self-respect. So if we feel more worthwhile as a result of being around someone, that is an important reason for wanting to prolong that experience — and vice versa.

Disloyalty takes many forms. At the low end of the scale we have those who simply do not do their share to uphold their end of the relationship. I am always skeptical of the arrangements people come up with to insure that the mundane maintenance tasks that absorb so much of our energy are equitably distributed. Sometimes lists and contracts specifying who does what are involved. But it is true that it is hard to live comfortably with someone who is unwilling to pull their weight in the housekeeping chores that few of us enjoy. At the other end of the scale is the deceit involved in having an affair. This particular form of disloyalty is intolerable to most of us since it violates the trust that is a fundamental component of the joint commitment two people have made to one another.

Perhaps we need to look at any relationship as a collection of implied promises. Foremost among these is an assurance not to do anything that would intentionally hurt the other person. The opposite of this promise-keeping is a kind of meanness that may manifest itself in "bickering" that keeps each partner in a defensive state of alertness. We all have seen situations in which continual disagreements, usually over small things, produce a pattern in which petty argument is the most common form of communication. If sarcasm also plays a significant role in the manner in which a couple talks to each other, this is an ominous sign for a continued connection. We all can absorb and accommodate disagreement from someone we love, but any expression of contempt, even (or especially) disguised as humor, is deadly.

A kind of mythology about relationships sounds plausible and is constantly invoked to justify all manner of conflictual behavior. It takes the form of a series of assertions that are accepted without question and that collectively constitute the conventional wisdom. "All couples fight," "It's better to get your anger out and not sit on your feelings," "Men only want one thing," "Women always have a hidden agenda," "Compromise is the secret to happiness," "Boredom is inevitable," "Look at nature, monogamy is unnatural." And so on. These truisms have the cumulative effect of keeping expectations low; as a result we settle for less than our deepest desires.

Finally, *danger lives at the extremes.* Freud famously inquired, "What do women want?" a question that has resonated with men across the years. The answer in matters of the heart, I believe, is that both men and women seek *excitement,* which is, after all, the precursor to behavior that fosters species survival. The problem for both sexes is that, like any mood-elevating drug, mindless excitement by itself frequently comes with some surprising side effects of the sort that we have already discussed.

The classic example of this phenomenon is the beautiful woman, accustomed to the attention of men, who wields her desirability as an instrument of power. Encouraged from an early age to use physical attractiveness to get what she wants (often starting with her father), she comes to value the superficial qualities that society associates with the feminine ideal. She is, in short, exciting. Her male counterpart, the seductive man, is equally skilled at generating enthusiasm in others, in this case, by projecting a potent mixture of success and vulnerability. Neither of these character types wear well over time since they have customarily not cultivated such traits as loyalty or reliability.

Of *boredom* this can be said: It is the primary underlying feeling in the litigants in most divorces. Often anger appears most prominent. But the anger is frequently a secondary response to the sadness and disappointment of unmet expectations. Look at the smiling bride and groom in their wedding pictures. Can you imagine that they will end up some years hence bored to distraction with each other? And yet the statistics do not lie; such is the fate of most couples. Familiarity, it seems, may not always breed contempt, but it infrequently nourishes attachment. If you are bored with your partner going in and married him or her for other reasons — security, family pressures, a fear of growing old alone — odds of prolonged happiness or a successful marriage are slim. Proverb: "The gods gave men fire and he invented fire engines. They gave him love and he invented marriage."

People to Cherish

The Essential Virtues

When we consider the characteristics and values that we seek in others and try to nurture in ourselves, some traits come immediately to mind. I have chosen ten virtues that I think most people would agree are important to pursue: *kindness, optimism, courage, loyalty, tolerance, flexibility, beauty, humor, honesty,* and *intelligence.* The list is not meant to be all-inclusive and you can doubtless think of other qualities that you value. In fact, doing so would be an excellent exercise. In some ways these ten virtues constitute for me the pinnacle of human aspiration. They are the antithesis of the selfishness, shallowness, discouragement, and anxiety that are the hallmarks of the disordered personalities that I have described in Part I.

I hasten to add that such distinctions are not meant to discriminate between mental health and mental illness, though a person possessed of most of the virtues I have listed is better adapted to living happily with others. In a larger sense, we can assume that a society that encourages people to manifest these traits will act in ways that emphasize collective objectives such as peace, reverence for the natural world, and regard for other people.

Like the previously discussed constellations of traits and behaviors that don't work, virtuous qualities tend to coexist predictably. People who place a high value on kindness, for example, are likely to be optimistic and tolerant, which are, after all, aspects of an outlook that intentionally respects the needs and desires of others.

It is also obvious that no one manifests every virtue in pure form. Indeed, some qualities like courage may come and go. No one is courageous in all situations, and there are different ways — moral, physical, intellectual — to be brave. So what we are looking for as imperfect human beings is someone who is making a sustained effort to behave in a fashion that displays as many of these virtues as possible. If we value such people, presumably we ourselves are trying to become one of them. The fact that we frequently fall short of the ideal is a test of the tolerance that is one of the core characteristics we aspire to.

It has been said that in life, unlike elementary school, no one awards grades for effort and only results are important. But given our shortcomings we must make allowances for difficulties in learning. Being a decent person requires a certain understanding of ourselves and others that only study and experience can provide. Just as we would not expect to demonstrate spontaneously the ability to speak a foreign language or ski gracefully, so we are engaged all our lives in the complex process of relating to other people. This is a task requiring a lot of self-study and learning from experience. Few formal courses are available and the quality of instruction from both our peers and those who have gone before is uneven.

If we must rely on our own observation of how the world works, we ought to take care to find people who embody the qualities we seek to develop. If we are lucky, our parents may serve as competent teachers and role models, but frequently we need to look elsewhere to find adults we admire. We have to trust that there is a body of knowledge about human relationships that we must master and that the best way to do this is by surrounding ourselves with those who believe it is possible to live intentional lives that contain both meaning and pleasure.

We are all works in progress, struggling to live well in a culture that often seems to reward narcissism and exploitativeness. If we want something different for ourselves, we need to learn how to recognize and draw close to similarly motivated persons who will support our efforts to become worthy of admiration. Among their number we will find those few who will love us and allow us to love them.

Kindness

Kindness is the indispensable virtue from which most of the others flow, the wellspring of our happiness. If the definition of love is raising the needs and desires of another to the level of our own, then kindness implies an ability to weigh these needs in every interaction with people. It assumes, but does not demand, that others will reciprocate and is in that way determinedly optimistic. It also reflects a belief in the essential decency of other human beings and so it must be tempered with an ability to recognize those who are unwilling or unable to respond and instead wish to take advantage of people naïve enough to believe that a capacity for kindness resides within each of us. The ability to love is not randomly distributed in the population and can be overwhelmed by a devotion to one's own self-interest.

Under its umbrella, kindness shelters a variety of highly valued and easily recognizable traits: empathy, generosity, unselfishness, tolerance, acceptance, compassion. Implied in all of these is the conviction that the quality of our relationships with other people is the primary determinant of our own happiness. Beyond that, however, is the belief that in our efforts to live successful lives we cannot do so at the expense of others. The notion of people prospering together is frequently submerged in the competition to achieve our share (and more) of whatever is valuable and advantageous to us: money, prestige, power. If these things are obtained by taking advantage of others, it is difficult to assign meaning to our lives that will sustain us.

We must be able in the end to reconcile our past behavior, derive pleasure from the moment, and envision a purpose to our future if we are to be happy. An ability to do all of these tasks requires that we learn to be kind. The linear narrative of our lives, past and future, viewed in the present, constitutes a story that we both write ourselves and contemplate as time rushes past. We want our tale to make sense, to express something about us that is uniquely valuable, that leaves some footprint in the hearts of those whom we care about. Few of us can take satisfaction from a life that does not include some sense that others have benefited from our time on earth.

To be in the presence of another person who accepts us as we are, gives us the benefit of the doubt, cares what we think, and assumes we will act generously is an immensely gratifying experience. We are drawn to such people, both because they are unusual and because they encourage us toward similar behavior. True kindness blurs the line between giving and receiving. It is the opposite of the "contractual" view of relationships in which we trade favors and keep score to ensure that we give no more than we receive. The latter construction, unfortunately, describes most marriages. Typically, the division of responsibility in such relationships is carefully negotiated so neither partner feels taken advantage of.

The point is that dissatisfaction with whatever bargain is struck is frequent and the subject of a lot of renegotiation in search of the elusive balance point of fairness. This need to be self-protective is burdensome and is the antithesis of a relationship in which kindness prevails. When I hear with some frequency from married people that they "love" their partner but "are not in love with them," I never know what to make of this distinction. It sounds as if people are talking about some obligation that they are forced to discharge without enthusiasm or excitement.

If kindness begets love, why is this virtue not more prevalent? The simplest answer is that we do not value kindness sufficiently as a culture. We are from an early age taught the importance of material success and encouraged to compete to achieve it. The multibillion dollar advertising industry bombards us with images that encourage dissatisfaction with what we have and how we look and perpetuates fantasies that we can purchase some better version of ourselves. Implied in this view of the world is that we must win a series of competitions involving academic success, occupational achievement, and status-enhancing relationships. In each of these areas we are expected to compete as if we can succeed only at the expense of others. Is it any wonder, then, that our lives are guided by self-interest and a fear of failure? Our attitudes toward relating to others are shaped by a similar apprehensive striving, which is why our mating dances are so complex and fraught with mistrust.

Picture the alternative. In the presence of one disposed to kindness you will notice an absence of guile, an ability to listen, and a disinclination to compete. If you can reciprocate, you will experience a growing feeling of safety and trust. You may find yourself disclosing things about yourself that you have previously been at pains to conceal: fears and vulnerabilities. The need for self-protection drops away, as does the requirement to appear to be something other than you are. You experience, paradoxically, a growing satisfaction with yourself combined with a desire to become a better person. You feel that a great burden has been lifted from you. You are, at last, good enough. In fact, the image of yourself that you see reflected in your loved one's eyes may be nearly perfect. You would like this moment to last forever. Imagine that.

Optimism

What is it that allows some of us to be hopeful in a world full of tragedy and injustice, where time and chance have their way with all of us, and where we face defeat in the end? Apart from a comforting religious faith, some trick of the mind is required to be able to derive pleasure and significance from the moment. Not everyone can do it. The lifetime prevalence of depression in the population has been estimated at 15–20 percent, while at any given moment around 10 percent of us are so beset by sadness and loss of personal significance that we qualify for a formal diagnosis of depression.

Given the state of the world, it is hardly surprising that many people harbor doubts about the future. Pessimists, those most prone to depression, almost invariably consider themselves realists, and watching the news it's hard to argue against the proposition that things are bad and getting worse. And yet our individual happiness in the present moment is largely dependent on what we anticipate. Our beliefs about the future constitute self-fulfilling prophesies; *we get not what we deserve but what we expect.*

This truth can be seen most vividly in our interactions with other people. Those we approach with trust and openness tend to respond helpfully. Conversely, if we treat people with suspicion, they are likely to reciprocate.

To be hopeful is not unselfish. On the contrary, it is in our self-interest to risk the occasional disappointment that optimism implies to benefit from the more frequent experience of realized hopes. The habitual mask of the pessimist is similar to that of the depressive: a fixed frown of discontent and unhappiness. In fact, the triad of perfectionism, pessimism, and discouragement is a familiar precursor to and accompaniment of clinical depression. The logic is unavoidable: Those who demand too much of themselves and others are bound to be unhappy in an imperfect world. Like most emotions (anger, anxiety, love), unhappiness is contagious; it feeds on itself and demands to be shared. There is a story of two girls assigned to clean a stable. One focuses on the material she is shoveling; the other thinks, "There must be a pony around here somewhere."

Like many of our attitudes, hope or the lack of it is, to some extent, a product of our experience. An area of psychology called "learned helplessness" concerns itself with the consequences to people when they conclude that they have little choice in what happens to them. If we assume that our efforts are unrelated to the outcomes in our lives, we develop an outlook of pessimism and passivity. Optimism requires that we believe that we can favorably influence our fates.

How we react to setbacks in our lives is a particularly good test of how hopeful we are. If we see some bad outcomes as being inevitable in a world in which our control is limited, we can nevertheless retain our confidence in our ability to change things for the better. If we react to adverse events by feeling discouraged and powerless and engage in a process of self-blame, we are unlikely to imagine that we can improve the situation. Eventually, our skepticism about changing things for the better hardens into an habitual attitude. Or as one bookstore visitor said, "I almost bought a book about how to think positively, but then I thought, 'What good would that do?'"

It usually doesn't take long to find out whether you are in the presence of an optimist or a pessimist. One of the best indicators of how someone else is feeling is the mood they evoke in us. If being around certain people causes us to feel discouraged, it is a fair bet that this is, at least in part, a reflection of their outlook. Conversely, optimism is also contagious. Sometimes this takes the form of a reinterpretation of events. Recently I was on a tour bus whose driver was the recipient of the truck driver's salute from an irritated motorist. Rather than express anger or insult, the driver suggested, "Look. That guy thinks I'm number one." As with all of life's adversities, a working sense of humor is an invaluable defense. The situation may be critical but not serious.

Optimism is highly correlated with success. What do you suppose a major league hitter is telling himself before he bats? Even the best of them make an out two-thirds of the time. Do you suppose that this statistic is weighing on him as he approaches the plate? Or is he likely to be imagining a happier result? People who never developed a belief in themselves, no matter their intrinsic talent, are unlikely to appear on major league rosters; they have long since been encouraged to pursue other occupations. The same might be said of successful salespeople. There is also a role here for recognizing that, since our pasts are largely stories of our own creation, we have the power of selective recall. Optimists are more likely to remember good outcomes while pessimists are discouraged by memories of failure.

On a hot day many years ago, my then–middle school daughter, Emily, one of the most optimistic people I know, was paddling with me in a cardboard boat race. As we began to take on water and the boat dissolved beneath us, I thought of the hours I had spent sealing and painting the fragile craft to prevent this outcome. Finally it sank and we became swimmers. Emily, seeing my disgust, said to me, "Oh Dad, doesn't that cool water feel good?"

The school of "positive psychology" has demonstrated that optimism, like helplessness, can be learned. Using cognitive techniques and stress management, Martin Seligman and his colleagues at the University of Pennsylvania have shown conclusively that pessimists can be taught to be optimists, with beneficial effects on school and occupational success, even health.

In one of the frequent examples of overlap between virtues, optimism is heavily dependent upon courage. Pessimism, like depression, is a safe position. Pessimists may be discouraged but they are seldom disappointed. If situations turn out badly, they expected as much. If things go better than predicted, they can only be pleasantly surprised. Optimists, on the other hand, risk disappointment, or worse yet, being taken advantage of and looking foolish. This is why we seek the middle ground, presumably occupied by true realists. Since we lack the power of foresight, however, we are all subject to surprise. So who would you rather spend your life with: those who brace themselves for the worst or those who anticipate the best?

Courage

There are many ways to be brave. The easiest to recognize is a willingness to take physical risks that most people would not consider. One of the salient characteristics of all creatures is behavior that conforms to a desire for self-preservation. This tendency is virtually an evolutionary imperative, to survive and reproduce. So what is it that impels some people to risk their survival on behalf of others or even in the name of an idea? This is the form of courage most often rewarded with medals. In combat soldiers are expected to be willing to sacrifice themselves for the mission or for the welfare of their comrades. Those who perform actions requiring exceptional bravery receive special recognition. (If you throw yourself on a grenade to spare those around you, you will likely be awarded the Congressional Medal of Honor — but only if the grenade goes off, in which case your family will receive it for you. If you pick up the grenade and throw it back, you get points for quick thinking but no medal.)

One of the many reprehensible things about war is

that conflicts are instigated and directed by the old but the sacrifices required are borne by the young. It seems particularly disingenuous to depend upon the idealism and good intentions of one generation to satisfy the aspirations and rectify the mistakes of their elders. All wars are simultaneously stages for heroism and brutality. The rationale for fighting is universally characterized as "freedom," our own or someone else's, even as we are aware that the underlying reasons are resources, territory, religion, or fear. In any event, those who bear the battle are never those who start the war or who benefit from it. Not in this century or the last.

The essence of courage is overcoming fear. We appear to be so in need of heroes these days that anyone who puts on a uniform or performs competently is accorded hero status. Gone is the concept of choosing to assume a risk on behalf of another. A pilot of a crippled airliner who is able to bring it safely to earth has done his job with exceptional skill, but he had no choice and is therefore, by my definition, not heroic. Someone who accepts the risks of military service or firefighting and survives is lucky but may or may not have performed heroically.

We tend to become confused by the adulation we lavish on those who entertain us. The accomplishments of athletes are highly rewarded, and we are prone in our celebrity worship to confuse actors with the characters they play.

In the more prosaic world of daily life, we are seldom required or given the opportunity to be physically heroic. Stories of civilian self-sacrifice tend to center on those who are persistently helpful to others: parents of handicapped children, people who do charitable works, those whose primary gift is their time, sometimes, as with Mother Theresa, their whole lives. Generosity (another word for kindness) rather than risk is the standard by which such acts are judged.

Then there is moral courage, in which people stand up for a deeply held, often unpopular, principle at significant cost to themselves. Here we have those who resign their jobs rather than compromise their ethics, those who refuse to remain silent in the face of injustice, those who act to protect the powerless. Again the element of risk and sacrifice is what distinguishes this sort of courage from simple altruism.

A closely related trait is *resiliency*. The ability to sustain the inevitable blows that life deals each of us and respond with a determination not to be defeated is one of the highest forms of courage. Unimaginable loss is all around us. Try to visualize a meeting of The Compassionate

Friends, an organization for parents whose children have died. Here one finds ordinary people trying to retain their grip on themselves and reality in a world that has taken from them a precious child through disease, accident, suicide, or murder. Parents newly bereaved, shocked and distraught, struggle to come to terms with the permanence of their loss. They turn for hope to the only people who can truly understand what they feel, other parents whose children have died. They are trying to hold on to their sanity, to regain some sense of themselves as having a future without their lost child. How long will they feel this way? How long before the lacerating open wound of their grief becomes a scar they will bear forever? Will they ever regain a sense that their lives have meaning? Can they possibly retain a belief in a benevolent God in the face of such an apparently meaningless catastrophe?

We all have our breaking points, the moment when we surrender even our self-respect to the pressures of fear or the random fate that threatens to crush us. Those who can hang on the longest earn our respect. Perhaps the most implacable enemy we confront in our lives is time, which slowly strips us of our youth and health, eventually robbing us even of our memories. ("Time is the school in which we learn; time is the fire in which we burn.") This is why growing old is for most of us simultaneously an exercise in cowardice and courage and why those who are young wish, usually in vain, for those who are old to provide some example of how to age with grace. In some ways the aging process is among our last chances as human beings to be brave and to give hope to those who must follow.

Another aspect of courage is a capacity for commitment. This ability to persist is in contrast to the more common tendency to give up when faced with fear or discomfort or lack of immediate success. When one is trying to assess the presence or absence of courage, especially in the young, their record of commitment to some person or activity can be a useful indication. The opposite, of course, is the chronic boredom that is such a common adolescent characteristic. With the advent of television, computers, and high-stimulus electronic games, it appears that our inability to entertain ourselves without technical support has markedly increased. There is a distinct difference between what we learn from reading a book and the lessons taught by playing Grand Theft Auto.

How is it possible, then, to know early in life, when we feel like we will live forever, who is courageous and who is not? It is a hard virtue to recognize because it has so many forms. Those willing to take physical risks, for example, may not display fidelity to an ideal or a willingness to sacrifice for another. And those who are brave for a moment in their youth may crumble beneath the awful weight of time. Nevertheless, courage and resilience are such important attributes, especially compared to the posturing of those who have never been tested, that they are worth looking for in people with whom we hope to spend the rest of our lives.

Loyalty

We live in a world that worships flash. We are drawn to bright colors and to people who dazzle us with displays of beauty over intelligence. We pay a lot of attention to peacocks and not as much to draft horses. The cultural icons who populate our magazine pages and movie screens and athletic fields are rewarded far beyond any discernible contributions to the welfare of others. It is natural to crave diversion but the disparity between what we pay our entertainers and what we pay, for example, those charged with educating our children is a dramatic testimony to what we value.

Observing what traits are exhibited (or uncommon) in those we most admire is illuminating. It could be argued that the characteristic least likely to be observed in this group is loyalty. For one thing, they are unburdened by anticipation that their marital habits will demonstrate a capacity for fidelity or longevity. A part of their obligation to entertain us apparently means that they are never off duty and their private lives are chronicled by our agents of gossip and candid photography. The contribution of celebrities to this process often appears to involve a requirement to behave as bizarrely as possible, sacrificing both their dignity and any vestige of propriety by abusing substances, wrecking cars, engaging in all possible forms of hedonistic behavior, and demonstrating a stunning lack of concern for those whom they marry or parent. While such behavior is not universal among movie stars, one is left with the impression that the incidence of loyalty among them is lower than in the population as a whole. Insofar as we admire their work and long to be rich and famous ourselves, it is hard not to imagine that the example set by these people establishes some sort of standard for the culture as a whole.

The days when we began and ended our careers with the same company are long past. The average length of time that people remain in a given job is now less than five years. The median length of marriages that lead to divorce is eight years. Even with the advent of recycling, we continue to live in a disposable society. The world is littered with our obsolete electronics. In a society where the concept of "new and improved" holds sway, the ideas of reliability and commitment have an almost quaint feel.

Deciding what and whom we choose to be loyal to is an exercise in priorities. Years ago I was drummed out of the military during the Vietnam War for being disloyal to my commanding officer. In my response to the efficiency report that ended my career, I listed my ascending priorities as follows: "I am a soldier, a physician, a citizen of the United States, and a free man upon the earth." For me the last three components of my identity outweighed the first; the Army, not surprisingly, disagreed.

The essence of loyalty is a willingness to keep one's word, but it is the failure to do that with which we are most familiar. What we are told by people trying to get elected may later appear to have been lies, but "inoperative statements" and unkept promises are most often simply declarations that are convenient at one moment but discardable later. They represent a form of moral relativism in which a longing for things like wealth and power takes precedence over values such as steadfastness or commitment. In fact, loyalty, whether it be to other people, institutions, or to the truth itself, can seem a prosaic impediment to getting what we want.

At a personal level, however, fidelity and dependability are indispensable to the intimacy we all seek. We cannot be close to anyone on whose word we cannot depend and whose promises we cannot believe. Flexibility usually accompanies tolerance, another essential virtue. But if a willingness to change becomes the rudderless course of least resistance, navigating toward a desired goal or maintaining a close relationship with those who depend on us is difficult.

The criteria for determining loyalty at any age are answers to a series of straightforward questions: Does this person consistently tell the truth? Is he there when you need him? Does she keep her promises? Are you confident that he will never intentionally hurt you? Does she behave as if you are at the center of her life? Do you, in short, trust this person completely? And does he evoke in *you* an effortless determination to be trustworthy?

Tolerance

What the world needs now may indeed be love, sweet love. Personally, I'd settle for a little more tolerance. Most of what we suffer from, most of what we fear and feel threatened by these days are people operating under the belief that they belong to a group that has a corner on the truth about human existence. And this "chosen" status requires them to convert or kill those who disagree. It makes no difference to a true believer that one's convictions about how to live and what deity to worship are largely an accident of birth and require no evidence beyond some book of doubtful authorship. This is called "faith," and the conflict it fosters may yet be the death of us all.

Something about the human condition makes us prone to organize into groups. Family and tribal loyalties, adaptive for survival in eons past, have become the bane of a shrinking world, where our capacity to inflict violent death on members of other tribes threatens to outstrip the capacity for cooperation and shared fate on which our survival depends. We have lived for more than sixty years under the shadow of nuclear annihilation and still we lack the imagination required to peacefully resolve differences. The primitive and oversimplified concept of evil has made a comeback as a political and theological construct. The idea that all human beings carry within them a capacity for both generosity and destruction strikes a little close to home for many of us who feel more comfortable imagining wickedness as the province of others while congratulating ourselves and those who believe as we do on our fundamental goodness.

Intolerance depends on a black-and-white view of the world and the people in it. This position is encouraged by binary tendencies in a society where competition is enshrined in our definitions of success (winners and losers). This is why intolerant people tend to be obtuse and why such sentiments are so often correlated with a lack of education. It is no accident that we have only two major political parties and why those most concerned with telling other people how to live, whether through legislation or exhortation, are frequently disposed to narrow-mindedness.

Confusion arises when those who are intolerant make a pretense of humility. It is impossible to be simultaneously humble and confident of exclusive salvation. One must beware those who pretend to know God's will or who are overly fond of punishment as an instrument of control. People who believe that it is legitimate to hit children, for example, are simply acting on their conviction that we are all born with a set of impulses and desires that render us selfish and that we must be disciplined from an early age to behave acceptably. (The hypocrisy behind efforts to control our own unacceptable impulses is on frequent and amusing display.)

Americans live in a society that imprisons more of its population (two million at last count) than any other. We also have more guns in circulation than any country in the world. A majority of our citizens continue to support the death penalty. Do you detect a pattern here?

A hallmark of intolerance is the assumption that those who disagree with us should be the objects of coercion. It is ironic that those who argue against the interference of government in the private lives of its citizens should simultaneously argue that their own view of the world should be codified and enforced as law. The right to be left alone is fundamental to a democratic society. At a personal level, intolerant people are quick to judge others and contemptuous of those who differ with them. In general, they make harsh parents. People certain of their own rectitude tend to be more attached to ideas than people.

Those who display tolerance are slower to judge others, particularly for behavior that, whatever the Bible or the Koran might say about it, does not harm other people. (One of my favorite cartoons shows one member of the Taliban saying to another, "Granted, actual music is a no-no, but where do we stand on air guitar?") Empathy, the ability to put oneself in the position of another person, is a fundamental component of tolerance, as is the ability to forgive those who have trespassed against us. To be tolerant is to believe in the idea that justice must be leavened with mercy and that revenge, while momentarily satisfying, is neither a viable foreign policy or a prescription for interpersonal success.

Tolerant people also tend to be better at that most difficult form of forgiveness, that which we must direct toward ourselves if we are to achieve anything like happy lives. We are all fallible, and if we cannot let go of past mistakes, we encumber our future with remorse. This is why tolerance is closely linked to optimism. People who are practiced at the task of forgiving themselves and others do not hold grudges. They travel light, unburdened by hate or regret, accepting the differences in people that make of life an endless wonder.

Honesty

The ability to trust another human being turns out to be a fundamental requirement for a lasting relationship. Confidence that someone is trustworthy takes time to develop, which is the reason that brief courtships so rarely lead to lasting marriages. Commitment depends on honesty, which is another reason for not joining your life to someone with a tendency to lie. That said, some lies are more important than others. Tactful falsehoods about hairstyles and clothes clearly do not carry the same weight as misstatements about feelings or fidelity.

Whether someone's word is dependable cuts to the heart of any relationship. Early signs that this might be a problem should be heeded. More than any other trait, the presence or absence of honesty, that is *integrity,* is a window into the soul of another person. Since nearly all of us know the difference between truth and lying, to choose the latter is an intentional failure that is overlooked at great peril.

Doctors are customarily held to an elevated standard

of integrity because their decisions can be so important to the welfare of their patients. What if the patient you are caring for is a wounded prisoner of war from whom your commanding officer wishes to extract information? That presents a conflict in loyalties, doesn't it? It did for me at least.

What about the pledges contained in our wedding vows? How binding are they as we and our spouses change over the years, even sometimes falling in love with other people? To judge by current cultural mores, the marriage contract is not as enforceable as, say, the loan agreements on our cars. (Another cartoon shows a husband saying to his wife, "I'm sure that 'till death do you part' was only an estimate.")

We have always been subject to deceit for profit or power. Who among us has not lied when it suited our purposes? Why should we be surprised when others play us for fools? While skepticism can serve us well, a cynical belief that we can trust no one is not an adaptive (or attractive) quality. This is why an expectation of honesty in people contemplating friendship, much less marriage, is crucial.

෴

Public lies dissolve the trust that enables us to live peacefully with each other. We need some reasonable belief that our news is accurate and our leaders are being honest with us to have a functioning society. Imagine what driving would be like if we could not trust our fellow motorists to stop at red lights and to drive on the correct side of the road. Governing consensus and enforceable law are impossible without a shared sense of trust. Every time one of our major institutions, especially our government, lies to us, there is a slight but progressive erosion in our ability to rely on each other. As with the "inconvenient truth" of global warming, we may end up drowning in a flood of cynicism and distrust.

We can all come up with examples that illuminate the perils of lying, cheating, and stealing in our personal lives. Every form of recovery, including psychotherapy, emphasizes the importance of being honest with ourselves and others. And we cannot live happily for long with people we cannot trust.

If you are looking to the next generation for help with constructing a more honest society, I have some bad news for you. A survey of thirty-six thousand high school students by the Josephson Institute of Ethics produced the following discouraging results:

- 60 percent reported that they had cheated on a test during the past year.
- 42 percent believe that a person has to lie or cheat sometimes to get ahead.
- 28 percent admitted that they had stolen something from a store in the past year.

And things may be even worse than these results suggest, since 27 percent said that they lied on at least one question on the survey.

Honesty with others is easier if we are accustomed to not lying to ourselves. It is possible to be both truthful and accepting at the same time. If we can look at our own strengths and weaknesses realistically but generously, we will be prepared to be straightforward with the people around us. It is a habit worth nurturing, and like forgiveness, it is a gift we give ourselves.

Beauty

Beauty is eternity gazing at itself in a mirror.
But you are eternity and you are the mirror.

—Kahlil Gibran

It seems amazing that beauty, which is such a subjective quality, should have become in our time so narrowly defined: a face with a certain symmetry, a body of a certain shape. So few of us can meet the standard, so few, no matter the content of their souls, feel beautiful in the eyes of others. Beauty becomes an accidental virtue, the result of good genes and little else.

Like intelligence, however, beauty manifests itself in many ways apart from physical appearance. People can demonstrate ugliness, plainness, or exquisite beauty in spiritual, intellectual, interpersonal, artistic, and emotional areas. To appreciate these qualities, however, requires more than a casual glance. It is common in college catalogs to see courses called "art appreciation" or "musical theory." These appear to promise, not that you will become more skilled artistically or learn to play an instrument, but that you will be better able to discern what qualities make one painting or composition "better" than another. Even though these are matters of taste, the assumption is that general rules exist about what can be classified as "art," that is, work that has some lasting value. (I note here that without a trace of irony, today's pop musicians, including the most profane of rappers, are referred to as "artists.")

We all understand the evanescence of physical beauty in human beings. "As we grow old, the beauty steals inward," said Emerson. What he meant was that certain attributes of character replace the good connective tissue that is the sole property of the young. These traits, fortunately for those wise enough to appreciate them, are usually discernible early in our lives, certainly by late adolescence. The problem for most of us is that we are too imperceptive (or uninformed) to recognize them, especially since we are blinded and deafened by our hormonal impulses and by the lopsided emphasis on physical attractiveness encouraged by our superficial culture.

Just as a morsel of food is beautiful to a starving person, our most strongly felt needs determine what and whom we are drawn to. If we require the admiration of others (and who does not covet this) and are uneasy about our own acceptability, we will likely conform our sense of what is attractive to the cultural norm. This may cause us to overlook the fact that conventionally beautiful people are frequently treated in ways that undermine the development of other characteristics that turn out to be more durable.

In the end we are forced to the realization that beauty exists at the intersection of the two great longings that dominate our lives: love and happiness. The mistakes in judgment to which we are prone are related to our under-developed ability to judge accurately who has the capacity and inclination to love us and who evokes similar feelings in us. Then there is the widespread confusion of the concepts happiness and pleasure; the latter omits the crucial component of *meaning* in any definition of what it signifies to be fulfilled over time.

We are genetically programmed to seek excitement; the survival of the species demands it. In the process we are drawn to certain people who induce in us feelings of desire. In many ways our responses to others are culture-bound and automatic. We are likely to focus attention to-ward similar images of physical attractiveness. We are in this way prisoners of our senses and subject therefore to mistakes about what we want and need. Whether we are able to see clearly with our minds and hearts, however, de-pends on whether we have learned what we truly require.

One of the things that makes this learning difficult is that the stories we are told, our cultural myths about what it means to be good, to be strong, to be smart, and to be heroic, are told by actors, people who embody the narrow but agreed upon standards of physical beauty. We are prone to forget that they are speaking words and expressing emotions crafted for them by others. (Why are there no photo spreads in popular magazines of the Writers Guild Award Show?) No wonder there is so much confusion about how to detect qualities such as intelligence or empathy and distinguish them from the superficial attributes that do not wear well over time.

We suffer mightily from this deficit in discernment. Our beholders' eyes are not equal to the task of separating gold from dross. We have, in effect, been trained to be insensible about the relationship between image and reality. We can overcome this disability only by learning through experience that our eyes do indeed deceive us and are unreliable guides to what we seek. The great deception is not just that we thoughtlessly adopt the societal consensus about what is beautiful. Our mistake is to neglect an unsparing inventory of our own desires so that we can recognize which of them are shallow and momentary and which are worthy of lifetime pursuit.

The urgency we associate with sex leads to all manner of terrible decisions. How much human tragedy is the product of sexual compulsion? We hear every day of crimes committed, careers ruined, and children damaged by those in the grip of impulses they cannot or will not control. From what source does this heedlessness and desperation emanate? How does the wish to control, dominate, and possess other human beings become so powerful that people will ruin themselves as well as those closest to them to satisfy this need?

And where is beauty in all of this? If people are drawn together by some shared combination of need and longing, how do we account for the fact that so often our choices are unsatisfying in the long run? Some believe that all behavior, even the most apparently altruistic, is the product of self-interest. Generosity, especially if publicly disclosed, is potentially self-serving. Only a small percentage of those who give to good causes choose to do so anonymously. Much of the money privately raised for the least fortunate in society comes from opulent events that are in part advertisements for the wealth of the donors. Does this make them any less generous or public-spirited? Perhaps not.

Still, this conflation of wealth, beauty, and charity further confuses those of us who are faced with the more mundane task of deciding whom we are drawn to. If lust for the perfect face or figure is an unreliable guide, what standard can we apply in choosing not just the person we want to sleep with but the one we want to wake up next to for the rest of our lives? I would argue that we need to look closely at another, larger question: When I am around this person do *I* feel beautiful? If the answer is "yes" (especially in the face of contrary evidence provided by any available mirror), something other than self-delusion may be occurring.

In fact, this question could be applied to any of the virtues we seek in others. The best indication that our search is over is whether we feel more inclined to exhibit these traits in ourselves. It is one explanation for the old saw that *like attracts like* (and a refutation of the equally well-known adage that *opposites attract*). It is not simply that we spend our lives with those in similar social, economic, and occupational circumstances and so are drawn to people who resemble us, but that when we spend time with others we become more like them. Just as soldiers can become brave by being with courageous comrades, so couples who have spent years in each other's company tend to share emotional, and sometimes even physical, characteristics. This is, perhaps, the best argument for choosing for a partner the person you want to become.

Humor

Our strongest defense against the fears engendered by our mortality is the ability to laugh. At the same time, this capacity is one of the most reliable ways of drawing people to us as we cope with our common predicaments.

A man wakes up in the middle of the night to discover that his wife is not breathing. He grabs the phone, calls 911, and explains the problem to the dispatcher.

"What's your address?" she asks.

"714 Eucalyptus Street," he replies.

"Can you spell that?" she inquires.

After a pause, the man says, "How about I take her over to Oak Street and you can pick her up there?"

A stand-up comedian says, "I want to die peacefully in my sleep like my grandfather, not screaming my lungs out like the passengers in his car."

Two people are in couple's therapy:

He: "One thing that bothers me is that you never tell me when you have an orgasm. "

She: "You're usually not there."

These three stories reveal some important truths about humor:

1. Brevity is essential. No good joke requires more than twenty seconds to tell. After that it's a shaggy dog story.
2. Familiar situations provide the best setup.
3. No subject is off-limits; everything is grist for the mill. Comedian Colin Quinn on the phenomenon of female suicide bombers: "With guys, they get seventy-two virgins when they die. But what do the women get? Seventy-two guys willing to discuss relationships and look through the J. Crew catalogue with you?"
4. Extra credit is given for jokes at your own expense. (Patient: "Oh, doctor, kiss me, please!" Psychiatrist: "That would be unethical. Actually, I shouldn't even be lying on this couch with you.")
5. Jokes should not be mean (unless they are funny). (Question: What's black and brown and looks good on a lawyer? Answer: A Doberman.)

It is obvious that people have different ideas about what constitutes humor. Some prefer sarcasm, others have an (inexplicable to me) affinity for puns. Still others like interminable stories, usually involving famous people, genies and wishes, or sexual double entendres. Like driving competence, everyone claims to have a good sense of humor. Often what is missing is an appreciation of the absurdity that underlies our lives and is a prerequisite to laughter. It is important to the longevity of relationships that those involved share a similar sense of humor. When all else fails an ability to make each other laugh binds people together. Here's an example.

Many years ago I had just returned from service in Vietnam, disillusioned by what I had seen there. I began to speak out against the war and was invited to be on a panel of veterans at Parkville High School in nearby Baltimore County. Those were disputatious times and when I finished speaking I was loudly booed by members of the student body. Fast-forward thirty-seven years and I receive an invitation to speak about the problems of aging at the Parkville Senior Center. When I told my wife of my long-ago experience at the high school, she said, "Great. It's probably the same people. They can boo you all over again."

The (relative) absence of a sense of humor is most revealing — and ominous. Extremely obsessive people lack the willingness to be surprised that humor requires. Depressed or self-consciously inhibited persons have difficulty in getting outside themselves sufficiently to laugh. Narcissistic, sociopathic, and histrionic people are often smart enough to be able to feign a sense of humor, but still their performances frequently lack conviction and spontaneity. The truth is that you don't have a sense of humor; it has you. Given the eventual tragedy of the individual human experience, all humor is gallows humor, laughter in the face of defeat. In this sense the ability to laugh requires courage. In the words of Mark Twain, "Humor owes more to sorrow than to joy."

When I was undergoing Army Ranger training many years ago, I remember the extreme stress, physical exhaustion, and fear that we could never show but that nearly overwhelmed us at times. One cold night our patrol was chest deep in a north Florida swamp, making slow progress while visions of cottonmouths and alligators danced in our heads. My Ranger buddy turned to me and whispered, "Are you sure this is the quickest route to Orlando?"

Flexibility

Life is continually presenting us with surprises, many of them unpleasant. People who like to plan and manifest a certain rigidity do not as a rule tolerate change well. We all know those who are easily thrown off stride by the unexpected. This trait is frequently correlated with a high level of impatience and irritability. In some ways a lack of flexibility can be seen as a relatively minor fault, except it expresses a great deal about such values as optimism and tolerance. It can also produce an atmosphere of tension in the people closest to us.

If it is true that "life is what happens while we're making other plans," finding ways of dealing with the unforeseen is helpful. Airports are good places to observe how people cope with unanticipated change. No one who has watched a long-suffering airline employee threatened with legal action by a disgruntled passenger can fail to be amazed at the inflexibility and sense of entitlement of some people. I always come away from observing one of these minidramas wondering how such a person would respond to *really* bad news.

Watching rigidity in action can teach us a range of undesirable traits: poor control of anger, an unattractive tendency to bully others, an inflated sense of self, and a lack of empathy for other human beings trying to do their jobs. If the hotel doesn't have your reservation, it is going to be difficult to assign responsibility for the mistake; however, the fault is unlikely to reside with the desk clerk whom you are berating. If your steak is not done to your satisfaction, by all means send it back, but insulting the waitress is unnecessary. If the person you are with has a tendency to do any of these things, think how he or she is likely to treat *your* mistakes over the course of a long marriage.

We want our partners to have a firm grasp on reality. In this case the reality is that life seldom goes exactly as planned. Things are lost, objects fall to the floor and break, children find ways to frustrate us. How we respond to these situations says a lot about us (not to mention the effect it has on the developing self-esteem of our kids). None of us wants to be hard to live with. Our capacity for flexibility has a lot to do with the way we are seen by others in a world of frequent frustration.

Intelligence

Most people have a pretty high, some might even say exaggerated, estimate of their own intelligence. If Lake Wobegon contains only children who are "above average," where, one wonders, are those who are below? How smart does our ideal spouse have to be? We all know about marriages across social classes, age disparities, and educational backgrounds. Who can say that love cannot transcend such differences? And yet the requirements of marital communication are such that we seldom see people with advanced degrees living with high school graduates.

So many things bring and keep people together that any obvious difference, such as race or religion, raises questions about long-term compatibility. Plenty of people have demonstrated the maturity to overcome such dissimilarities but, as noted, most people choose for partners people with backgrounds very like their own.

We are coming to realize that intelligence, far from being an easily defined number on an IQ test, takes many forms. Apart from so-called cognitive intelligence, we have emotional, artistic, physical, verbal, musical, mathematical, and other forms of talent that can be measured. Even so, when it comes to compatibility, the ability to frame and talk about the world with similar skill appears to be important.

Those inclined to think reflectively about their lives are especially likely to want to talk about these questions with someone, who, if he does not necessarily agree in all respects, can still hold up his end of a philosophical or political discussion. Those who manage to ignore such issues are unlikely to want to talk about them. In fact, a case can be made (at least by the content of most overheard cellphone conversations) that the majority of people are more concerned with the minutiae of their lives than weighing subjects of larger significance.

Nevertheless, however we distract ourselves, we are faced with the need to find something to do and someone to love. Especially as we grow older, these tasks take on increasing urgency, and however we try to concentrate on other things, we are forced back on what might be called a search for meaning. Once we get past feelings of sexual attraction or social status we encounter the realization that we are going to spend more time talking to our spouse than any other marital activity. Here is where the issue of intelligence comes in. It is difficult to have sustained conversations with someone whose interests are radically different than our own.

The standard assumption is that men have a gender-determined deficit in their ability to listen. And yet we all know that our inclination to pay attention to anything is a function of our interest in the subject being discussed. This is obviously a further argument for the importance of similar intelligence in couples who wish to keep alive their capacity for dialogue with each other. Most people report some drop-off in conversation with time. Whether their silence is companionable or simply the product of boredom is extremely important to the durability of the relationship.

So intelligence is included as a virtuous trait not because smart people have any better record of marital success. It is just another area in which people who are alike have a better chance at happiness together if they have more to share and an ability to communicate about subjects that they both find appealing, amusing, or otherwise interesting. If silence descends upon them, it cannot be hostile or despairing or the product of alienation. Our need to be heard, understood, and valued is so strong that we either have it or we must seek it elsewhere. When I hear stories about infidelity, novel sex is not customarily the driving force behind it.

3

It Is Not the Answer That Enlightens but the Question

The most dangerous food to eat is a wedding cake.

The long process of figuring out why we are often drawn to people who turn out not to be good for us leads us to the conclusion that something deeper is going on here, some rule of living that makes us want what we do not want. At first this may be perceived as a learning problem. Since we cannot predict future behavior with any accuracy, even our own, how can we expect the choices we make in our youth to be satisfying in our middle age? Much of the content of this book has focused on improving our decision-making ability by contemplating those traits of character that are likely to endure and cause us either endless joy or pain.

Even so, we must acknowledge that we regularly confuse pleasure with happiness and are as a consequence drawn to people and pursuits that provide us with more of the former than the latter. This tendency is sometimes described as hedonism, and the tension it creates between short-term and long-term gratification constitutes one of the recurrent themes of human behavior.

In its simplest form, the abuse of substances is a study in the hazards of immediate gratification. No one who has tried drugs can deny that they produce temporarily pleasurable sensations that most of us would like to repeat. It also becomes apparent to nearly everyone that long-term use results in unwanted, degrading, and soul-destroying outcomes that render us unable to function, the very antithesis of the pleasure we seek to replicate. We can label this "addiction" and turn it into a disease to diminish stigma and facilitate treatment, and yet we must admit that the misuse of substances is a manifestation of a larger paradox: *the mindless pursuit of pleasure brings pain.*

And so it is with relationships. Qualities that seem so important at one stage of our lives — physical attractiveness, the promise of excitement, social status — usually do not persist indefinitely. Some traits that do endure may not be so appealing in the long run, leading to disillusionment and confusion. Since we are bombarded by images of youth and beauty, it is easy to become confused about the value of more lasting qualities. Few magazines or television shows are devoted to telling the stories of people doing constructive work or living lives of fidelity and determination. Such people are seen as unexceptional and a little dull in a society preoccupied with entertainment. Just as the universal human tendency is to slow down to observe the carnage of an auto accident, so we will always be fascinated by misbehavior and other forms of distraction.

If we confuse success with fame and accomplishment with notoriety, we sacrifice any belief in the power of thought or reflection. One of the reasons why young people see going to school as an onerous burden is that the entertainment value of most instruction is very low, especially when compared to movies, video games, and other activities that occupy their free time. The boredom that characterizes school is good preparation only for work, which is commonly seen as an unpleasant necessity to generate the money needed to enjoy those possessions and activities that *do* bring us pleasure.

This perspective on school and work often includes the belief that satisfying our needs requires a tradeoff in which everything has its price. The implication is that every person has desires that may require some sacrifice from their partner who has requirements of his or her own. No one is expected to get everything they want, and achieving even partial satisfaction in the relationship requires a continual process of negotiation of differences.

This approach, although it meets some superficial test of fairness, is laborious and requires a lot of scorekeeping. With the advent of the women's movement in the last half of the twentieth century, it became an article of faith in some circles that "no one relinquishes power willingly." Much of the shift from the patriarchal system to greater equality was accompanied by competition in the relationship between the sexes, leading to an atmosphere of compromise and negotiation. A divorce rate hovering around 50 percent suggests, among other things, that these negotiations may not be going well.

Perhaps another model for success in intimate relationships might stand a better chance than the contractual approach currently in favor. What if your choice of partner involved an informed evaluation of their ability to give themselves generously to marriage? What if they expected only that their kindness would be matched by yours? Does this sound hopelessly naïve or difficult? Would such a person be defenseless and subject to exploitation? Your answers to these questions reveal a lot about you, your assumptions about the world, and most important, your estimate of your own ability to respond with a reciprocal and giving spirit.

The advantage of such an approach is that it provides a model for relating to another person that requires a lot less negotiation. The disadvantage is that you have to become both insightful about yourself and an exceptional judge of character since not everyone is capable of such emotional surrender.

There is a story about a man's lengthy search for the perfect woman. When he found her they could not connect since she was searching for the perfect man. This is the primary issue in constructing a relationship based on generosity and placing the needs of another at the level of our own. The question is not just where would you find such a person, but are you prepared to give what you wish to receive?

The gods too are fond of a joke: the role of chance in human affairs.

The conventional wisdom sold to us by the cult of personal responsibility would suggest that we all make our own luck. This leads inevitably to discussions about things like whether or not we are responsible if our plane is hijacked. Psychoanalysis, with its focus on the swamp of unconscious thoughts and feelings that have such an effect on our behavior, would propose that there are no accidents. While it is doubtlessly true that we are responsible for most of what happens to us, surely there is a place in human affairs for the inadvertent and unpredictable. When the only empty seat at that conference thirty-six years ago was the one next to my future wife, it is hard for me to deny that this was the luckiest thing that ever happened to me.

And yet there is some truth in the aphorisms: "Chance favors the prepared mind," "Fortune favors the bold," "The harder I work, the luckier I get." There is something to be said for preparedness in any discussion of human relationships. In a sense we can think of our lives as groundwork for the good things and people we will encounter. Still, whether we do encounter them involves a lot of luck. Our task when we are young is to become like the person we seek and put ourselves in situations where a meeting is apt to occur.

Meanwhile we are engaged in the other undertakings that complete our lives — getting an education, finding activities that cause us to lose track of time, cultivating habits that lead to energy and good health (and avoiding those that do not) — in other words, discerning how the world works. An important component of this knowledge is how to cope with the passage of time, especially the all-important process of knowing what to hold onto and what to relinquish.

Perhaps this latter skill, learning how to let go, will be most useful to us given the number of losses that we will be faced with. If we are lucky, the process will have some predictability. Our parents will predecease us; our children will not. Our bodies and minds will not betray us until near the end. Nothing catastrophic will happen before its time to us or those we love. We can hope, but always with the knowledge that what we control in these matters is significantly less than what we do not. And so we would do well to prepare ourselves as well as we can for the unexpected. Simply acknowledging the role of chance will enable us to be humbled without breaking.

Far too often we take credit for our good luck, which makes us vulnerable to later misfortune. Whenever I hear someone who has had something terrible happen to him or her ask the most pointless question in the world, "Why me?" I have the impulse to answer, "Why not you?" The implication on the part of those who are surprised at bad luck is that they have somehow earned their good fortune, which they expected to persist indefinitely. This attitude is of a piece with those who believe that because they are good people who have obeyed the rules, they will be rewarded. This, of course, is a subset of the myth that life is fair, or that God rewards us in accord with our devotion and worthiness. What evidence is there for such beliefs?

A better question when confronted with bad luck (or good luck for that matter) is "What do I do now that this has happened to me?" If our misfortune is great, the death of a child for example, it is easy to get stuck in our grief. We become like a soldier who has lost a limb, entitled to feel sorry for ourselves and with a need to grieve our loss for whatever time it takes us. Still the question hangs there, "What next?" How long we take to answer is up to us.

So luck is an ever-present force in our lives. It teaches us humility. No matter how hard we work, how much money we have, how important to us is control in all we do, still we are subject to the vagaries of chance. Only fools believe that they are the sole, or even primary, architects of their fates. We are subject to cancer, to car crashes, to wayward lightning strikes, and finally, to the ravages of time. What gives each moment its intensity is the knowledge that we are all hanging by a thread and the control that we work so hard to establish is an illusion, that the race is really not, in the long run, to the swift.

Love will make you forget time
and time will make you forget love.

Wealth and power are nearly universally admired, if not envied, especially in a society where few people feel heard or even visible except to friends and family. Why do people in crowds wave when a TV camera is pointed at them? Who are they waving to? How can people sign a release for their faces to be televised during the worst moments of their lives, while being arrested, for example? Why are there so many applications for participation in reality shows that carry the certainty of discomfort and humiliation? The answer, of course, is that being on television is a kind of affirmation that we exist and are visible, if only for a moment.

If, in our daily lives, we feel relatively unnoticed or powerless, the feeling is bound to affect our relationships with those around us. This is the source of many of the struggles that infect our marriages. Even the usual progression of love — from sexual attraction to infatuation to habituation to an unenthusiastic affection (often approaching boredom) — is a violation of our youthful fantasies about how the world should work. If this sequence is superimposed on the fears that inevitably accompany aging, the stage is set for a lot of discontent, if not anger. We feel in the grip of forces that we cannot control and wonder if *any* of our decisions about how to live have been good ones.

This somber backdrop explains why the "life is hard; you must negotiate to get what you want" school of thought is so popular, even if it plants the seeds of conflict with those closest to us. Negotiating is important when people have competing interests. When we buy a car, for example, we know that our desire for the lowest possible price diverges from that of the salesperson, who would prefer the highest. Since there is no emotional attachment between us, negotiation is appropriate. If there *is* an emotional attachment, if, for example, the salesperson is our next-door neighbor, the negotiation will probably be resolved in favor of the person who cares least about the other. This, not incidentally, is also true in many marriages.

This is why negotiation, particularly in an atmosphere of hostility and defensiveness, is such a blunt instrument of conflict resolution between people who are supposed to love each other. Why, then, is it such a widely recommended solution (on the part of therapists who should know better) to marital discord?

First, it sounds plausible. After all, isn't negotiation the answer to real-world problems ranging from preventing war to passing legislation to getting bargains at a flea market? Why doesn't it work better between people in long-term relationships? The answer is that few of the fights that couples have are about the topic that appears to be the issue. We are told that sex, money, and children are the most popular subjects for disagreement in marriages. And yet the repetitive nature of most marital conflict suggests that what is happening represents a kind of dance that is familiar and even reassuring to both parties right up until the moment one of them decides that they can't stand it anymore. Then comes the problem of explaining what went wrong to interested observers. There is something odd about the fact that falling *in* love requires no explanation but that we are expected to produce (or make up) a satisfactory reason for falling *out* of love.

What has happened in many marriages that end in divorce is that the relationship has gone from a cooperative enterprise to a struggle for power that neither party can win or resolve. The field on which this contest is fought varies from couple to couple and time to time. From the outside, the disagreements may appear to be bickering, but that word cannot encompass the strength of feeling that is evoked or the magnitude of the stakes — until the end. What is driving this conflict and impeding resolution is that the struggle eventually comes to be seen by both people as a battle for psychic survival in which their personhood, their worth as human beings, is the real issue. Once people decide that, they will usually but not always disengage. The alternative is to continue the familiar dance. I sometimes suggest to patients who decide to stay together in spite of chronic discord that they rent *Who's Afraid of Virginia Woolf* and watch it together. (It is illuminating that the stars of this movie, Richard Burton and Elizabeth Taylor, had thirteen marriages between them, including *two* to each other.)

As with all the mistakes that we are heir to as human beings, the only antidote to errors of the heart is to learn how to make better choices in our friends and the lovers they may become. Hint: Anything about the other person that annoys you will be magnified with the passing years (and vice versa). This is why the question of control is so important early in any relationship. Presumably, most people regard marriage as a cooperative undertaking. If the person you are considering appears to be highly competitive and preoccupied with issues of control, look closely at whether this need carries over into their interactions with you. This is one variation on the toxic traits that I described earlier in the discussion of self-absorption. You do not want such a person around your children, especially as a co-parent.

A typical plea from a woman seeking Internet advice goes as follows:

> When he gets angry at me, I stop talking and then we seem to disintegrate into snide comments, cold stares, and a distance that is fraught with tension. Eventually the yelling begins and the same complaints from both sides get repeated without any hope of ever getting resolved. "You are always down." "Well, you are always too frantic." "You complain about everything." "Well, you are always too busy to spend quality time with me." It just goes on and on until we are too tired to continue. At that time, I think we will never reconcile, but soon the argument is forgotten and we just realize that we love each other, that we have been together too long to treat the relationship lightly, that we have been through a lot together and that we will be together always.

Can these people stop such repetitive behavior? Possibly, but not likely since neither can see the power struggle that lies beneath their conflict.

Is it possible to construct a marriage that is relatively free of conflict? Expert opinion suggests no. Some competition and disagreement are widely believed to be inevitable, so that most advice on this subject is directed at compromise solutions and conflict resolution. The implication is that love has its limits. No one can care enough about another person to see their interests as equivalent to one's own *all the time.* We are all, it is assumed, prone to selfishness. To question this assumption is to imagine an unattainable perfection.

As long as expectations remain modest, we can anticipate modest results. If our model for close relationships involves a lot of self-protective bargaining, this is what we can expect. If the imperfections of our beloved become increasingly annoying over time, we can be sure of a reciprocal annoyance directed at our own shortcomings. If this results in mutual criticism and argument, we are exactly where we are supposed to be, exactly where our parents were, living out the marriage contract as fairly and resignedly as we can and congratulating ourselves if we manage to stay together. "What if this is as good as it gets?" Jack Nicholson asks a waiting room of psychiatric patients, a question that most couples should be asking themselves.

Any landing you can walk away from is a good landing.

When a plane crashes, the National Transportation Safety Board conducts a meticulous investigation to determine the "probable cause" of the accident. Was it pilot error, bad weather, or mechanical failure? If such an effort were expended to do a psychological autopsy on failed marriages, what would it show? The short answer is that we would probably see two people who were different at 40 than they were at 20; no surprise there. It would also uncover a lot of anger between them, some of it overt, much of it unexpressed. And what would people be angry about? "I didn't realize what sort of person he/she really was when we married." Closer questioning would usually disclose misgivings early in the relationship that were disregarded or interpreted as characteristics that would change with time and love.

Often the desire to marry is driven by timing, hope, and ticking clocks of various descriptions. Few people can exit their twenties unattached without some sense that they are on a different schedule than most of their friends. The urgency of this feeling varies, but it accounts for a lot of compromise decisions. When people come to me in the midst of a contentious divorce with complaints about their estranged spouse, here is what I often tell them: "Apparently you made the choice to marry this person who turned out not to be the man you thought he was. That was a mistake. Life usually requires that we pay for our mistakes. What you are going through now is that payment." This may seem heartless, but the truth often is, and self-pity at our own lack of foresight is seldom constructive and never attractive.

When I hear proposals for stabilizing marriages, such as a requirement for premarital counseling, I always wish someone would specify that if you get divorced you are required to reimburse your parents for the cost of the wedding and return the cash value of each gift to the giver. That might help keep people together — or at least give them pause before they walk down the aisle.

But I digress from our task of crash reconstruction, important only because of the fact that people seem to learn so little from falling in and out of love with such regularity. This lack of learning is evident from statistics that show that second (and third) marriages have a failure rate higher than our first lunges at matrimony.

If the cause of most marital discord could be encompassed by one word, I would suggest *criticism*. It is astounding how many reprimands, unwanted suggestions, and outright orders are exchanged by people who promised to love and to cherish each other. ("Obey" has thankfully fallen out of fashion in the recitation of vows, though people often behave as if it had been included.) Everything from passenger-side driving to demands for help with the children and the housework fall into the category of criticism. This is a variation of the nearly universal truth that "Nobody likes to be told what to do." Tone of voice and word choice are crucial here. There is a world of difference between a polite request for help and a querulous demand that implies that the other person must be bullied into lending a hand. When I gently suggest that couples try to dispense with criticism, most of them look at me as if I had proposed unilateral disarmament to the Secretary of Defense.

This is an indication of the self-protectiveness that permeates most bad marriages. The idea that you need to defend yourself from the person closest to you is the very antithesis of love and makes one wonder what could be the basis of any attachment between people who feel that way. Such an attitude conveys mistrust and, if it persists, is a precursor to a separation required to maintain one's sense of oneself.

Beyond the corrosive long-term effects of criticism is the related problem of other forms of conflict based on the desire for control. I mentioned that one of life's enduring paradoxes is that an obsessive need for control leads to interpersonal isolation and loss of control. Or, put another way: When it comes to relationships *we gain control by relinquishing it.* Naturally, this can occur only when we feel safe and loved.

If we learn early in our lives to choose our friends carefully and if we develop certain traits that we admire, we become eligible to meet someone who will engage with us in the infinitely satisfying dance of reciprocal love. Implied in the process of finding such a person is a lot of luck and a lot of patience. (Malcolm Gladwell suggests that it requires ten thousand hours to become "expert" at anything.)

As long as we believe that any choice we make is going to involve a compromise between an unattainable perfection and a tolerable reality, the more we will be inclined to settle for someone less than our deepest desire. Since we are acutely aware of our own imperfections, we are inclined to overlook or accept the shortcomings of a prospective partner, never asking ourselves whether we will be so charitable after living with this person for a few years. By the time we realize we have made a mistake, enough has happened (house, children, the investment of time, the weight of long habit) that we frequently feel both trapped and angry, ready for some first-rate marital therapy. Here we are likely to be fed a dose of the standard wisdom about the hard work of relationships and the importance of negotiation skills.

Perfect people exist. Not necessarily perfect by any objective standard but perfect for us (or perfectible *with* us). If we are insecure (and who is not), they are reassuring. When we display impatience, they are tolerant. If they are fearful, we can be brave. What really characterizes such a relationship is a virtual absence of criticism, conflict, struggles for control, or a sense that either person must give something up to get what he or she wants. In fact, in a good relationship, the line between giving and receiving is blurred and the idea of intentionally hurting the other person is unthinkable.

Does this appear to be asking too much? Is the lesson of life really that we always have to settle for less than we want? That nothing or no one can meet our fondest hopes? Beliefs such as this, reinforced by seeing people all around us compromise in every area of their lives "as we all must," cause us to be cynical about the possibility of enduring love. The fact that we long for a transcendent experience is visible in the rapture on the faces of worshipers at charismatic churches, secure in the love they feel for God, who loves them unconditionally in return. This faith is rarely replicated in our relationships with other people. How can this be? Perhaps because none of us can promise each other life everlasting. All we *can* promise is to have and to hold until death do us part, a vow frequently made but less often realized.

Falling in love with love
is falling for make-believe.

Even the phrase itself, falling in love, suggests that one is helplessly, if delightfully, out of control when we are infatuated with someone. It is as if the meaning of our lives has become suddenly clear, we are experiencing an emotion that will last forever, and something has come to us unbidden. Although we know that this is a routine event that has happened billions of times before to others, why then do we feel uniquely blessed?

We are aware that in the end, everything that transpires in our brains is the product of some chemical process, a set of neurotransmitters released, some electrical activity in our limbic system. To protect ourselves from this knowledge, we invoke the heart, which is transformed from an organ responsible for the circulation of blood to the center of our affections that resides somewhere adjacent to our equally elusive but supremely important soul. The fact that these perceptions of joy, passion, and immortality can be mimicked by the ingestion of various illegal substances should be a tip-off that something chemical is at work in our brains. I mention all this not to rob love of its power and mystery, but as a reminder that these chemical surges by which our emotions are mediated are subject to change without notification and need to be informed by the reasoning ability that resides in our cerebral cortex.

The experience of being smitten by another human being commonly occurs for the first time as a teenager before we have much real experience of the world and the people in it. In fact, this emotion has a name, puppy love. The feelings evoked by this phenomenon are no less strong than with the adult variety. It's just that teenagers are believed to be less able to make lasting and intelligent decisions about themselves or others, so that few of these infatuations progress to permanence. What does happen in these experiences, however, is that one retains a memory of how wonderful it felt, and, like a drug, the process of falling in love can promote an addiction that lasts into adulthood (tempered modestly by the recall of the pain of breaking up).

The basis of infatuation varies widely between people, and surveys show that men and women in general are looking for different things in prospective marriage partners. Most often the source of male attraction is physical beauty, whereas women tend to be looking for a good provider and prospective father. In this atmosphere, a lot of room exists for misunderstanding and competing needs. There is the added burden that men are customarily socialized to compete while women are expected to do most of the heavy lifting involved with processing emotion. This may sound like a stereotype, but most therapists would, I think, attest to the different communication styles exhibited by the genders. (A cartoon shows a couple sitting outside their cave. The title is "The emergence of language." The woman is saying, "We need to talk." The caveman is thinking, "Uh-oh.")

The problem with the process is not just that men and women have different incentives to create a relationship or even that they communicate differently. The problem is that people of both genders are unskilled at looking beneath the surface to discern those qualities, in themselves and others, that last. In fact, the power of infatuation, whatever its basis, is strong enough to overcome rational thought, hence the truism, "Love is blind." Even after the heedless, live-forever days of adolescence, many people remain sentimentally attached to fairy tale endings.

The real questions about love hover somewhere between rational evaluation and chemically mediated lunacy. Most of us, when we are offered the ecstasy provided by cocaine or heroin, will decline because we have observed the drawbacks of addiction. But addiction to love has such a good reputation that it appears safe. Only in extreme cases will anyone dare to say to someone in love, "I don't think this is the right person for you." Who has the courage to even try to puncture someone else's affectional balloon?

And so the stage is set for the mistakes that occur when we choose impulse over reflection. Besotted, we decide to link our lives to people we know only in the most superficial ways. Next, the marriage process itself takes over and proceeds through engagement, the expensive and prolonged rituals of wedding planning, to the day itself in all its splendor. And then we begin the frequently surprising task of getting to know the other person. All the usual antidotes to this sequence of events have proven futile. There is little evidence, for example, that couples who live together before marriage do any better than those who don't. Length of engagement is similarly not correlated with marital survival. We are apparently as poorly qualified to make predictions about someone else's future behavior as are psychiatrists in predicting dangerousness in their patients.

What can we conclude from all this beyond the facts that life is full of surprises and few of us display the gift of foresight? One answer is contained in the following story.

A man walking down a dark street at night comes across another man on his hands and knees in the gutter searching for something under a streetlight. "What are you looking for?" asks the man. "My car keys," the second man replies. "Let me help," the first man says as he gets down and starts to look. After a few minutes he asks, "Are you sure you dropped them here?" The other man replies, "Actually I dropped them half a block back." "Then why are you looking here?" the man inquires. "Because this is where the light is," is the answer.

Likewise, searching for love in the wrong place or hoping to evoke it in the wrong person seldom produces lasting happiness. Jumping off a dark cliff may feel like flying for a moment, but it can be risky if you cannot accurately anticipate a soft landing.

This is where learning comes in. If you have a clear idea what character consists of and what qualities in other people you need to pay attention to, you are much less likely to make the catastrophic mistakes that now plague the institution of marriage. Life has no guarantees, but why we pay less attention to this body of knowledge than we do to learning algebra is a persistent mystery.

Experience:
Test first, lesson later.

In our efforts to transmit to our children information that will be useful to them in later life, we tend to focus on conventional subjects like math, history, and writing to prepare them for the next level in their educations. Few people are satisfied that we are doing an excellent job at this, and we are forever bemoaning the fact that other countries do it better. For a long time I have believed that we ignore completely instruction about human behavior and personality traits that would contribute to the happiness of our children. Because a discussion of values would be a part of such teaching, educators are understandably leery of giving offense to parents who presumably are in charge of this segment of their children's educations. It is clear, however, from things such as teen pregnancy statistics, drug abuse rates, and above all, divorce statistics that something is lacking in the preparation of adolescents to form lasting relationships and live satisfying lives.

So perhaps it would not be out of the question to construct some courses under the general title of "Barriers to Happiness" (or perhaps "How to avoid people who will break your heart") to consider these issues. If it is legitimate to try to teach teenagers the importance of maintaining their physical health, why not spend an equivalent time talking with them about their emotional health, how to recognize in others the qualities that make people suitable or unsuitable for long-term relationships, and how to nurture desirable traits in themselves? Our silence on these subjects simply guarantees that all learning in these areas will be guided by peers and involve a lot of mistakes.

How about a course in "Characteristics of a good marriage partner?" Since finding such a person is highly correlated with future happiness and we are, collectively, doing such a poor job of it at present, wouldn't it be worthwhile for adolescents to contemplate such virtues as kindness, tolerance, and capacity for commitment and learn how to both recognize and cultivate these traits?

Simply defining the terms of such discussions would be valuable. What constitutes happiness and how do people define it in their own lives? What is the definition of love, one of the most ambiguous and misused words in the language? How do we tell whom we should be wary of and whom we should draw close to? Is monogamy a natural and satisfying part of the human condition? What are healthy and unhealthy ways to resolve conflict? How do we confront and deal with our mortality? How do we cope with loss? What is the role of sex in our search for lasting happiness?

It is amazing how little instruction adolescents have to guide them. Beset by the demands of their developing bodies, preoccupied with a sense of sexual urgency, fearing the rejections that inevitably await them, confused about what it means to be a successful man or woman, confronted with cultural paragons of beauty to which they cannot usually aspire, they understandably have little confidence that either parents or teachers have much guidance to offer.

It is not surprising that most parents fall back on a series of restrictions and proscriptions, things one *must not do,* relating mostly to drugs, sex, and driving. It's as if our fears for our children's survival overwhelm our sense of what they need to navigate happily through their lives.

I think young people would respond with interest to these subjects. My experiences with teenagers in therapy is that they generally value the chance to have a conversation with a thoughtful, nonjudgmental adult about subjects germane to their daily experience.

We have a lot to overcome in establishing such a dialogue. Years ago Simon and Garfunkel wrote a song called "Kodachrome." One of the lines was, "When I think of all the crap I learned in high school, it's a wonder I can think at all." Much of what we now teach our children is irrelevant to their future success as human beings and they know it. Think what their lives might be like if we could give them information and engage them in discussions that were applicable to their lives now and that improved their chances of future success in their pursuit of happiness.

We could have guest speakers at these courses: Couples who still love each other after fifty years together, couples who fell out of love quickly, people who are dying, people whose happiness flows from their religious faith, people who believe that God is a myth. Just the process of considering such issues might encourage habits of thinking that teenagers could use later when confronting that most important task of attaching meaning to their lives. Even Hollywood could be enlisted by the use of films that consider serious questions about how to live (*Ordinary People, On Golden Pond, Fatal Attraction,* and *Shallow Hal* come immediately to mind). Why not give it a try? Think how much the teachers would learn.

*The trouble with parents is that
by the time they are experienced
they are unemployed.*

Not all parents are created equal. The ideal of unconditional parental love is not available to all of us; some people seem incapable of such emotion, often because they never experienced it from their own parents. Few training programs exist in how to be a good parent, and even if there were, it is fair to say that one person cannot teach another how to love.

What we are left with then is a lot of people who fall back on on-the-job training and their own reservoirs of kindness and responsibility. If these reservoirs are depleted by external circumstances, such as marital discord, lack of good role models, the demands of work, or other children to care for, it is not surprising that many young people will be neglected emotionally or suffer the lasting pain of parental rejection or abuse. Children raised in such an atmosphere do not enjoy the benefits of a secure attachment to their parents, which serves as a shield from the vagaries of affection, given and withheld, lost and found, that we all experience in life. Children who have been loved unconditionally by emotionally healthy care-givers typically retain a good opinion of themselves for a lifetime, in spite of the losses and rejections they may face.

Our first experience of the all-important virtue of empathy comes from our earliest experience as infants, before we are able to use words to communicate our needs. This is why the standard advice to parents to "let the child cry until he falls asleep" is so puzzling. It is as if it is important to convey to babies that they cannot manipulate us, that they must be trained to endure discomfort lest we "spoil" them. In fact, all that is being taught by such withholding of attention is that the needs of the parents take precedence over those of the child. This is not likely to increase any child's sense of security or teach him what it means to be loved.

As the child becomes mobile and begins to explore the world, we encounter yet another bit of mythology. This is the period that parents refer to as the "terrible twos." Because the demands for monitoring increase, the stage is set for power struggles in which the word "no" begins to play an enhanced role. Rather than using distraction or preventive measures such as childproofing the environment, many parents see the child's newfound independence as a potential threat to their authority and believe that this is a suitable time to establish who is in charge. In many ways, these struggles serve as precursors of adolescent conflicts to come.

It seems ridiculous in the twenty-first century to be talking about the disadvantages, not to mention immorality, of physical discipline directed at children, but such punishment persists in some homes and still finds its defenders in spite of laws to the contrary. The instructive value of violence against children is an absurd concept. Among the saddest words I hear in therapy are, "My parents spanked us and it never did me any harm." The confusion attending this linkage of violence and love is confusing and leaves lasting scars across the generations.

Since children are small and relatively helpless in the face of parents determined to assert their control, they frequently respond with so-called passive-aggressive behaviors in which they exercise their limited power by persisting in unwanted conduct. Not surprisingly, parents find this infuriating and redouble their efforts at control. Once this dynamic is established it can lead to endless reprimands and years of frustration and resentment on all sides. As children grow in this atmosphere, they become more adept at frustrating parental attempts to lecture them about what they should be doing, as if this were a learning problem rather than a power struggle. By the time they reach adolescence, the stage is set for major conflict.

The risks of developing a passive-aggressive style have been discussed previously. It is a poor way to relate to authority and can ruin the lives of those who employ it, not the least by making them poor candidates for an intimate relationship. The number of families who get caught up in these repetitive and pointless interactions is astonishing, but if parents feel relatively powerless to control their own lives, they often bring their resentments home and express them in unimaginative efforts to control their children.

There is a universal idea that, by virtue of being cared for when young, children incur an emotional debt that they must spend their lives discharging. Even though becoming a parent is an adult decision, a common belief is that our children *owe* us respect and obedience regardless of their competing needs to build their own lives. This idea is so pervasive that people now in middle age frequently feel guilty about not being attentive enough to their parents. Often this obligation takes the form of having to listen to endless complaints about the infirmities of age and being chastised for not visiting or calling enough.

Relationships based on obligation are seldom satisfactory. Love and respect are gifts that must be freely given. And actions performed out of guilt beget resentment on both sides. We hold most people in our lives responsible for sustaining their end of whatever relationship exists between us. If they are boring, demanding, and full of complaints, they are unlikely to be our friends for long. And yet because someone has given birth to us and cared for us while we were young, we feel duty-bound to indulge them as they become cranky, self-absorbed, and shaming in their interactions with us. Who made that rule?

We can all agree that old age is difficult. To deal with the inevitable losses of aging requires a high order of courage and grace. None of us is sure how we will handle this stage of our lives until it becomes our turn to do so. Does that mean, then, that senior citizens, especially those we are related to, are given exemption from the social imperatives that bind us together in relationships of choice? Are we no longer required to be considerate of the needs and feelings of those younger, including the need not to be bored to death? Do those who love us as we grow old have an endless requirement to indulge our bad moods? Are we now freed from the usual requirements of friendship, much less love: to attend to the needs of other people and to not be so self-absorbed that we no longer know how to listen? And, more especially, are our lives now so hard that we are entitled to employ accusations of inattention as a means of chastising those who care about us?

Good parents raise their children to leave them. This is why one of the indicators that a family is not working well is that the adult children are still at home. It appears sometimes that there is an agreement in such families that the children will not separate until all the unresolved conflicts from earlier years are worked out. This frequently lengthy process is usually explained on economic grounds ("Joey is just saving for a house"), but the root of such a prolongation of childhood is most often a mutual fear of separation.

We all carry our parents within us. If they have loved us and prepared us to live independently in the world, we are fortunate and they are deserving of our undying gratitude, freely given. If what we feel for them instead is some mixture of resentment and obligation, we are in need of a process, therapeutic or self-taught, that will enable us to forgive their shortcomings and think about what we need to do to meet our obligations to *our* children, now and when they are grown and we are old.

If it weren't for marriage,
men and women would have to fight
with total strangers.

We have looked at some of the ways we can reliably evaluate other people's weaknesses and strengths. If we can identify those most likely to break our hearts and if we learn those traits of character that qualify people for committed, long-term relationships, we will have taken a giant step toward insuring our future happiness. We are then in a position to surround ourselves with people who will nurture our own efforts to become the person we want to be while increasing the chances that we will link our future to someone able to reciprocate our love. But the nature of the relationship that we expect to form is important to define.

The traditional view of marriage is that it is an institution that rests on an implied contract. Before the 1960s the exchange went roughly as follows: The man's responsibility was to provide an adequate family income while his wife supplied housekeeping and child rearing services.

Access to sex was an ancillary part of the bargain, but who that benefited the most varied. Responsibility for decisions affecting the family also differed widely from couple to couple, though the default position reflected the patriarchy sanctioned by most religions.

With the advent of the women's movement and the growing economic advantage of both parents working, there was a gradual, if largely unspoken, evolution in the terms of the marriage contract in the direction of gender equality. As women became less submissive, the marital ideal shifted somewhat, though less than you might think, in the direction of sharing household responsibilities, including more paternal involvement with children. That this shift in assumptions about marriage paralleled an increase in the rate of divorce can be seen as the inevitable "good news, bad news" quality of most changes in life, whether individual or societal. The military has a principle called "unity of command" (meaning someone has to be in charge), which is considered essential for success in war. When this tenet was violated in marital relationships, conflict increased.

What has replaced the ideal of benign paternalism in marriage, is touted in most books on the subject, is the concept of negotiation of differences. This view rests on two apparently indisputable assumptions: Nobody's perfect and all relationships require "hard work" to develop and maintain. (I think of this as the ditch-digging school of marital advice.)

Who can argue that when two imperfect human beings join their lives there are bound to be differences in what each wants, enjoys, and is repelled by? Usually, any household has tasks that neither party enjoys: cleaning, laundry, taking out the garbage, and changing diapers come immediately to mind. How do partners with equal time and equal status decide who does what? Assuming that such questions will be negotiated (and renegotiated) in the interests of fairness and harmony is natural. One can suppose therefore that one of the things that makes any relationship hard work is the strenuous and self-protective pursuit of that elusive balance of unwanted responsibilities.

Note that conflict over such issues is expected, hence the truism that "all couples fight," which led to one book of marital advice being titled *How to Fight Fair.* So the conventional wisdom revolves around the ideas of conflict resolution and compromise. This approach sounds logical, but the fact that about half of married couples can't stand each other after a few years of living together should raise some questions. Surely the majority of them were smart enough to know what they *should* be doing but for some reason could not negotiate their way out of an inconvenient fact: *They no longer loved each other.* In fact, if what happens in most divorces is any indication, they had come to actively dislike each other. And who among their wedding guests could have foretold it?

If you believe in the sanctity of marriage, you will probably suggest that they just didn't work hard enough. Or they lacked the requisite negotiation skills. Or they never learned to fight fairly. Or they unexpectedly fell in love with someone else. Or they grew apart. Somehow none of these explanations seems to capture what has happened in a collapsed relationship.

The one thing we can say about every broken marriage is that there has been a *failure of expectations* on the part of one or both parties. (Often overlooked is the reality that, while it requires two people to construct a relationship, it requires only one to destroy it.) And then there is our lack of foresight. Few of us anticipate that we will always look the same as we do in our wedding pictures, so why are we so frequently surprised when we change in other ways?

Nearly every divorce is marked by a long period of gradual alienation between the parties. The initial bickering and disagreements often precede the wedding. The "cold feet" phenomenon in the days leading up to the ceremony is well known. Sometimes the misgivings take the form of, "Sure we seemed to fight a lot and I was worried about his drinking, but he was okay most of the time and I thought, 'Nobody's perfect.' Besides, the invitations were sent, the reception was planned and paid for. I couldn't imagine backing out. Everyone told me we made a great couple." I'm accustomed to hearing this story from people of both genders who are in the midst of a divorce.

A declining marriage is an exception to the general rule that in life we get not what we deserve, but what we expect. At the beginning most people have a sentimentally optimistic view of what their marriage will be like. Living happily ever after is not just the ending of many fairy tales; it is the best hope of most couples at the moment they decide to join their lives for better or for worse. Nobody expects the worse, much less the worst. Even though most of us have been witness to unsatisfactory marriages, often in our own families, we tend to think that things will work out differently for us. (This assumption always reminds me of words attributed to the novelist William Saroyan on his deathbed, "Everybody has got to die, but I have always believed an exception would be made in my case.") As an exercise, try counting the number of successful marriages you have encountered, those in which people have not only stayed together over a long time but who appear to genuinely still like and respect each other. The unfortunate thing about marriages that turn sour is the intervening illusory hope that "perhaps having children will bring us closer together."

Life can be seen as a series of disillusionments. We relinquish the tooth fairy and Santa Claus early on. Our hopes for fairness in this world seldom survive our teenage years. Still many of us cling to a belief in the power of our love to change other people and are shocked when this turns out not to be true. No one says to us when we are young that we must learn how to evaluate other people's character so that we can distinguish those whom we can trust. No one points out the red flags that alert us to personality traits that are signals of future betrayal. No one describes in any systematic way the virtues we need to develop in ourselves so that we can recognize them in others. And no one questions the conventional model of relationships as requiring hard work and continual negotiation.

Beware of those
who are sure they are right.

Implied in our choice of people with whom to share our lives is a set of values that expresses but goes beyond the individual traits of character that we admire. Our concept of what it means to be generous, or empathetic, or honest, for example, underlies our every action toward our fellow human beings and informs our choices about how we organize as citizens to govern ourselves and relate as a nation to other peoples.

It seems simple enough to say that no country, no faith, no political party has a monopoly on the truth. All the ways in which we separate ourselves, all the tribes we are born into or choose are at risk of claiming exclusivity when it comes to their beliefs about how to live. If we could only stipulate that *no one knows* the answer to certain ultimate questions: What happens to us when we die? Have all questions about right and wrong already been answered by a divine being? Or are they uniquely human ruminations that flow from the struggle to impose order on the chaos of competing needs in a world that would otherwise simply favor the strong over the weak? Why should we be good?

This is not a book about politics or religion, though these turn out to be important subjects to consider when one is thinking about choosing someone to love. People have successfully married across the barriers of race and faith, though usually not without some difficulty. The same could presumably be said for differing political beliefs, especially if neither person cares much about the subject. If they do care, however, it is hard to imagine that cohabitation would not produce conflict.

The best advice for people with strong feelings about matters of faith or social issues may be not to get emotionally involved with those who have very different opinions about such matters. It must be strange to live with a partner knowing that you will cancel each other's vote in the next election. But perhaps if there were more marriages of this sort that worked, we might see why "Love conquers all" is more than a cliché.

Money can't buy happiness;
it can, however, rent it.

Of all the things that cause conflict in long-term relationships, money — how it is earned and how it is spent — is one of the most common and in some ways the strangest. It is fair to assume that in most such disagreements, money is a stand-in for more difficult-to-discuss areas of marital life. Nevertheless, some conversation about and observation of your partner's attitude toward money is prudent before marriage. (We have previously discussed the contrasts between generosity and obsessiveness.) Wealthy people would seem to have an advantage here, but it turns out that the correlation between wealth and happiness (or marital success) is very weak beyond some minimum point in which families are above the poverty level.

Usually, both partners work. This relatively new development in marriages has led to some interesting variations on money management. If there are disparities in income between people who are married, some decision needs to be made about who pays for what and whose money is whose. Some couples find it easiest to pool their incomes in a joint account and free themselves from the scorekeeping required if expenses need to be divided equitably. Frequently, there are separate accounts with separate credit cards for which the partners are individually responsible. A discouraging though inevitable development, especially in the case of second (or third) marriages, is the rise of prenuptial agreements in which each partner's limited obligation to the other in case of divorce is spelled out. These contracts, struck at the moment one is about to promise a lifetime commitment, imply a lack of trust, both in one's own judgment and in the promises that one's partner is about to make. Given the previous experience of divorce and the desire to secure one's fortune for one's children, it is perfectly understandable that one would seek some financial protection. Yet there is something symbolic about requiring the person you love to sign a document that promises not to steal from you. Not a hopeful way to start a marriage, I would say.

Since we live in a materialistic society in which the nature of the lives we lead is to a large extent determined by how much money we have, it is not surprising that this is the field on which so much marital conflict plays out. For the majority of people who have some uncertainty about the significance of their lives, material possessions are one way to gauge success. We are in many ways preoccupied with fantasies of unlimited wealth. The lines that form when lottery jackpots grow large are a testimony to the hope within us that our lives can be transformed without effort.

When there are marked differences in how two married people regard money, the stage is set for chronic conflict. What is being worked out are differences in personality traits of the sort we have previously considered, particularly the need to control versus resentment at being controlled. In marital therapy this is the issue that most often emerges when couples begin to discuss monetary differences. Typically, one person in the relationship will overspend while the other carps at them for being irresponsible. What often ensue are conversations about compromise, budgets, and cutting up credit cards. But these apparently sensible solutions seldom work because they do not address the larger power struggle that exists in the relationship and is usually expressed in other areas of disagreement as well. Until people confront these, all the budgeting in the world will not avail them.

Money can also serve as a symbol of or substitute for love. The child of wealth whose material needs are met or exceeded while they are left in the care of hired help is a cultural cliché. Even in families of more modest means it is possible to shortchange children in the areas of attention and affection while seeing that they do not want for food or shelter. Both situations are a form of parental neglect that leaves children feeling devalued in a way that permanently distorts the meaning of *both* love and money. Parent-child bonds are formed in the messiness of dirty diapers, shared dinners, and help with homework. Material possessions cannot fill the gaps left if these responsibilities are not met.

When we encounter people who were deprived of a sustaining relationship with at least one parental figure, we need to consider closely whether this deprivation has had a harmful effect on their ability to feel good about themselves, a prerequisite for sustained good feelings about others. When one is disadvantaged in this way, it often creates a symbolic hole in one's character that requires strenuous and long-lasting attempts to fill. Common ways of trying to repair this lack as adults include substance abuse, unreasonable demands upon and mistrust of others, and a peculiar relationship to money and the things it can buy. There are now twelve-step programs for compulsive shoppers. While this condition has not yet been dignified with its own psychiatric diagnosis, its consequences can be as destructive as other forms of substance abuse.

Whatever our childhoods were like, we all develop a characteristic attitude about money. For some it becomes a measure of success or a means of keeping score in the game of life. While most people find their sense of worth tied more to the relationships they form and the importance they attach to their work or free time, for others money is a continual source of worry and getting more of it can be a preoccupation and cause for frustration. Some choose to live in ways that allow them to ignore money completely and pursue happy and parsimonious lives serving their faith or cultivating their own gardens. Wherever you fall on this continuum, it will behoove you to choose for your partner someone with an attitude toward money that is similar to yours. The alternative is a lifetime of conflict and anxiety.

Ideas are easier to love than people.

There are a number of activities that people engage in because they are more attached to the idea of doing them than the activity itself. If you go to any ski resort you will discover those who spend more time in the lodge than on the slopes. Some people join yacht clubs primarily for the social opportunities rather than the sailing, which can be strenuous. Certain pursuits, especially if they require skill or effort, are more appealing in the abstract than in the reality.

And so it is with people that we get attached to. Not only is it difficult to know another human being as they really are (much less who they will become), we are all prone to imagining that we have discovered the person who will fulfill our dreams as a partner, complement our weaknesses, and save us from loneliness. *Readiness* is the characteristic that makes us most vulnerable to idealizing a prospective mate. We are each on different schedules of need. Traditionally, women were expected to marry in their late teens or early twenties. With more career op-

portunities now available, the average age at first marriage has climbed to twenty-five and a half for women
and twenty-seven and a half for men. Most see this
change from marriage at younger ages as a development
that will decrease matrimonial mistakes because of a pre-
sumed increase in maturity and life experience among the
newly married. But these numbers also suggest that people in their late twenties are aware that they are dropping
behind their age cohort in the marriage sweepstakes and
this may affect their readiness, not to mention eagerness,
for a permanent relationship. This increase in readiness
may be associated with a vulnerability to idealization and
a concomitant decrease in discrimination.

If this is true, and especially if we lack the insight to realize this development, we are apt to fall in love with the
idea of the person we are with and overlook the characteristics that render him or her a risky choice of partner.
Most people I talk to, especially women, who are over
thirty and single have plenty of experience on which to
base their evaluations of potential mates. I hear a lot of
generalizations, most negative, that begin with the words
"All women" or "All men." These statements have a defensive quality, as if they were being offered in response
to an unspoken question, "Why aren't you married yet?"
The people who tend to actually put this into words are

one's parents or oneself. Most of us would like to feel that we are hitting life's milestones at roughly the same time as our contemporaries. How many weddings in which we have been bridesmaids or groomsmen does it take before we feel the burden of dropping behind?

This whole issue of choosing the right time to marry is one of life's many and enduring paradoxes: *If we marry young we may be too immature to make a sensible choice of partner; if we wait too long we may make a poor decision out of desperation.*

Who says God doesn't have a sense of humor?

A wish to catch up, conscious or unconscious, is usually combined in women with a realistic fear of declining fertility. This may be postponed somewhat in men, who are more likely still to see themselves eligible to marry a younger woman, but the thought of "How old will I be at my child's high school graduation?" affects both genders. I remember vividly the first time I was mistaken for my youngest daughter's grandfather.

The process of idealization involves a tendency to shut down one's capacity for discernment and may result in ignoring misgivings about one's prospective partner that deserve attention. The fatal flaw of self-absorption becomes a source of admiration for self-confidence. An affection for intoxicating substances becomes a quirk that will yield to love, children, or increasing responsibility. A need to control will surely with time dissolve into a realization that compromise is the soul of marriage. And so on.

Nobody gets through the day without a rationalization or two. When choosing someone with whom you expect to share the rest of your life, however, ignoring real character flaws is beyond dangerous. Decisions made in a time when one is feeling even a little desperate are less reliable than flipping a coin. Whatever one might say about love, it cannot be deaf, dumb, *and* blind.

If you were arrested for kindness,
would there be enough evidence
to convict?

Happiness has many definitions. Each person is free to adopt his or her own. However, most people pursue certain goals: an income that allows them to live comfortably, health as good as their genetic heritage allows, and a lasting and dependable relationship with at least one other human being outside their family of origin. In achieving the latter of these three objectives, we are given little formal instruction. Most people learn by trial and error, an approach that has several drawbacks.

First is the element of risk. Our initial attempts to discover whom to draw close to and whom to be wary of take place in adolescence when we suffer from a surfeit of hormones and a dearth of experience; our bodies are more mature than our brains. The result is that our first close relationships, however promising they may seem to us, seldom endure. Often we remain puzzled about the transitory quality of these experiences and imagine that our uncertainty about such matters will magically be resolved in adulthood.

Another thing that we are not taught as children is that much, perhaps most, of our behavior is driven by unconscious needs and impulses rather than being a product of considered thought. In fact, nothing in our early schooling provides us with information about the psychoanalytic concept of unconscious processes, so we are left without a way to look below the surface of our lives (and the lives of others) or to come to grips with any concept of the way human personalities develop and manifest themselves. This educational deficit is seldom remedied in early adulthood, when we are making consequential decisions about falling in love, marrying, and having children. The results of this lack of knowledge are evident in the failure rate of these choices.

We each have a finite, though unknown, time to experiment with relationships. And we are confronted with a dearth of insight into our lives that compromises our ability to understand our mistakes in judgment. Usually, these errors involve an inability to perceive what another person is like in any complete way, their strengths and weakness of character and how they match our own. Most of us are aware that people change over the years, but we are not very adept at discerning the qualities in each of us that endure (in spite of the folk admonition that "Sex is for a little while; cooking is forever.").

Part of this failure in the ability to judge others is a lack of awareness of the truth that the best indicator of a connection between us and another person is *how we feel about ourselves in their presence*. While this may sound narcissistic, it is a window into our unconscious reaction to them. Recall the heart-stopping quality of Jack Nicholson's compliment to Helen Hunt in *As Good as It Gets*: "You make me want to be a better man." If someone can evoke this feeling in us, we are truly in love.

And yet many people take as a life lesson the idea that love does not last, that the best we can hope for is serial monogamy. What people are referring to is the fact that infatuation does not last. The heady, passion-driven form of temporary insanity that we associate with early attraction is for most people evanescent (though it has been known to persist for some lucky couples). It is hard to live with someone for many years and remain blind to their imperfections. However, the comfortable pleasures of mature love are many and in some ways superior to that intoxicating, desperate early attachment. Those who do not know this are prone to try to seek the novel experience of falling in love over and over, usually with unhappy consequences.

To be eligible for a lasting and mutually satisfying bond with another person requires considerable maturity, an ability to know what qualities of character are complementary to our own, and a lot of luck. We may be aware of the desirable traits we seek in the person of our dreams, yet not have the good fortune to meet him or her. In this case, depending on the depth of our insecurity and loneliness, we generally settle for someone less qualified, to our lasting regret. If, however, awareness is combined with patience, we may succeed.

The world is populated by many beautiful people. It is hard to credit the notion that there is one person perfect for us. What is more likely is that people who have the right combination of love and discernment *become* perfect for each other together. The connections we form involve a process in which the tenuous bonds of physical attraction are strengthened by shared experiences of pleasure and sorrow, and finally by the love and grief and hope that bind us irrevocably to each other.

With a little bit of knowledge, effort, and luck this destiny can be yours.

ॐ

It is in the nature of love that it eludes explanation. After all the attempts to rationalize it in terms of mutual need and shared interests, we still lack the ability to describe why two people feel themselves drawn to each other in a fashion that defies rationality but is, while it lasts, the most powerful force in the universe. In an attempt to explain the unexplainable, people speak of "chemistry," that indefinable variable that separates friendship from love. Like all forms of experimentation with chemicals, there is the risk of mistakes that can sometimes be explosive. If what we are hoping for when we join our life to another's is an enduring commitment, statistics suggest we will be wrong more than half the time.

What can we do to improve the chances that the attraction we feel when young will persist when the sex becomes routine and the flaws of our beloved have all been exposed? When our good looks have fled and when the dreams of our youth have dwindled, how can we keep our disappointment with ourselves from spilling over onto the person who has been witness to all of it, who is a constant reminder of the losses we have suffered, and who may have turned out to be less persistently enamored of us than we had hoped?

The bond that appeared so romantic in the early stages of our relationship has changed into a kind of open-eyed realism; the longing we felt has been replaced by a combination of obligation and convenience that seems more like a contract for services than a promise of undying delight. Perhaps our future lacks hopeful anticipation and we come to believe that most of the surprises that await us are likely to be bad news.

Am I being unduly cynical about marriage? Look around you at people who have managed to stay together for more than twenty years, whose children are grown and who now are confronted with thirty or forty years with only each other. I read recently the obituary of a man who died at seventy-six. Among his survivors was his wife of fifty-five years from whom he was divorced the year before he died. Did he complain too much about his final illness? Did she fall in love with someone else? Or did they do something they had been contemplating for decades but had kept putting off?

And yet we all know of good marriages that have both endured and remained satisfying. The nature of the attraction may have changed, but what remains can legitimately be characterized as love and the ties that bind them together consist of a sense of shared fate that has endured through the pleasure and pain of their years together. These are mature attachments that depend in equal parts on the character traits of both parties, especially kindness and loyalty. Were these values discernible when they first met? How were they astute enough to see in the other person this capacity for commitment? Perhaps they were just lucky.

We all have undiscovered abilities. When we are young and untested, they may not be apparent or perhaps simply not valued. When I was in high school it was considered good sport among the boys to make fun of the elderly janitor who cleaned the school. One of our number, who was something of an outcast himself, refused to participate and, in fact, went out of his way to be kind to the old man. It wasn't until much later that I came to know this person, now grown, and observe the man he had become. It became apparent that his capacity for generosity still exceeded our own and he was living a rewarding life: a good career, attentive friends, a satisfying marriage. It had been right in front of us all the time had we had the eyes to see. I told him so at our last reunion; he looked at me with surprise, both that I remembered and as if it had never occurred to him to behave otherwise.

We stumble through life without the owner's manual that we should have been issued at birth. We try to discern how to get our physical and emotional needs met. We attempt to learn from our frequent and painful mistakes. We suffer the sting of rejection and loneliness. And through it all we try to discover whom to avoid and whom to cherish as if our very lives depended on it.

꒰ꩄ꒱

We also struggle to a greater or lesser degree to make sense of our existence. I have listened to many people talk about the ways that their searches for happiness and meaning have gone awry. Some of them appear to have had some biological basis for their discouragement or anxieties. More often, however, they have been trying to answer important existential questions having to do with why we are here and what we must do to meet our responsibilities, live honestly according to our best conception of the truth of our existence, and increase the ratio of pleasure to pain in our lives.

This I have come to believe is the human condition: uncertain, confusing, often absurd, and full of anxiety in the face of an indifferent universe that can, and frequently does, crush our best hopes and dearest loves. Still we push on into a future we can neither imagine nor control, with nothing to guide us but some words we share with each other and a faith that we are not alone.

About the Author

Gordon Livingston, M.D., a graduate of West Point and the John Hopkins School of Medicine, has been a physician since 1967. He is a psychiatrist and writer who contributes frequently to the *Washington Post, San Francisco Chronicle, Baltimore Sun,* and *Reader's Digest.* Awarded the Bronze Star for valor in Vietnam, he is also the author of *Too Soon Old, Too Late Smart: Thirty True Things You Need to Know Now; Only Spring: On Mourning the Death of My Son;* and *And Never Stop Dancing: Thirty More True Things You Need to Know Now.* He lives and works in Columbia, Maryland.

Visit *www.gordonlivingston.com.*